DESIREÉ
HOPE YOU ENJOY
MY LATEST BOOK AS MUCH
AS WE ENJOY YOUR
WINES
ALL THE BEST

BRAD LUCAS
2020

PRAISE FOR

"*Pulling Profits* gives you the measure of your company – because what gets measured improves. Brad Sugars and Monte Wyatt have crafted a deeply insightful process for building sustainable success, and for creating an organization where people are engaged, empowered and committed."

Robert G. Allen, *New York Times* bestselling author of **Creating Wealth, Multiple Streams of Income** and **The One Minute Millionaire**

"Profit is not just money left over from sales and operational costs – it's the reward for a job well done and a plan well executed. It's where hard work meets team-work. And it's the value you create that adds to your growth and legacy. *Pulling Profits Out of a Hat – Adding Zeros to Your Company Isn't Magic* is a gem. A 10-carat diamond in the rough. All you have to do is take it for yourself and craft your own jewel. Monte Wyatt is a world class business coach and profit generator. Brad Sugars is a world class entrepreneur and wealth generator. Learning from these two you can't go wrong."

Jeffrey Gitomer, author of **The Little Red Book of Selling** and **The Sales Manifesto**

"In *Pulling Profits*, Brad Sugars and Monte Wyatt show how every single person in a company is vital to its success. *Pulling Profits* provides a disciplined and exciting approach to build on the untapped potential of a business. Brad and Monte take us through their customized steps to ensure that all constituents of an organization – the company, the customer, the team member, the stakeholder and the community – understand and contribute to creating magic to add zeros to the bottom line. Everyone who wants to achieve exponential business growth needs to read this book."

Dr. Ivan Misner, founder of **BNI**

"*Pulling Profits* reveals how to identify new income streams by pulling enormous wealth out of overlooked areas of your business. Using their vast experience as two of the world's leading business and executive coaches, Brad Sugars and Monte Wyatt offer a system to help you achieve sustainable, exponential growth in all levels of your organization. They provide definitive action steps to fix what needs help, and even to vastly improve what's already working well. *Pulling Profits* is a handbook for building a sustainable business."

Sharon Lechter, CPA CGMA, author of **Think and Grow Rich for Women,** co-author of **Outwitting the Devil, Three Feet from Gold, Rich Dad Poor Dad** and 14 other books in the **Rich Dad Series**

"*Pulling Profits* uses Brad Sugars' and Monte Wyatt's vast experience and deep insights from their work with ACTION Coach to create a handbook for continual improvement at all levels in a company. *Pulling Profits* offers tools for finding the magic that leads to positive change – including powerful self-assessments that will prepare you for strategic planning. You'll learn how to focus on the job at hand as well as future goals – and create balance in your organization. It's a real breakthrough among business books – wise and inspiring, with clear-cut action steps for measurable results. I can't recommend it highly enough."

Dr. Tony Alessandra, CEO of **Assessments 24×7 LLC, NSA Speakers Hall of Fame** & **Legends of the Speaking Profession**

"We live in a tumultuous age, with business owners everywhere looking for a way forward. Brad Sugars and Monte Wyatt provide a roadmap. *Pulling Profits* focuses on what makes a successful business: the people in it and how they work together and serve others. Through their insights into human nature and profound understanding of society and community, Brad and Monte have created a surefire classic on building a thriving business."

Michael R. Drew, bestselling author of **Pendulum: How Past Generations Shape Our Present and Predict Our Future**

"How do you build a sustainable company? How do you create exponential growth? Brad Sugars and Monte Wyatt know how. In *Pulling Profits Out of a Hat*, these topnotch business and executive coaches have turned their wide-ranging experience into an extraordinarily detailed program for business success. It all starts by placing people over profit, and building from there."

Aaron Scott Young, CEO, Entrepreneur, Creator, **The Unshackled Owner Program**

"*Pulling Profits* will open up your eyes to the greatness you've got in your business – but that you don't yet appreciate. Brad Sugars and Monte Wyatt have combined their awesome business-coaching talent and experience to create a handbook for exponential growth. They give you tools to sharpen your insights so you can take advantage of the potential you've already got in your organization. You'll find steps to develop the people, the talent and the potential of everyone who works with you. *Pulling Profits* is chock full of wisdom, humor and the kind of practical information that will make you say, "Now, why didn't I think of that?" Well, Brad and Monte did – and thanks to their book, you can start pulling profits right away."

Trav Bell, founder & CEO, **Bucket List Coaches**

"*Pulling Profits Out of a Hat* shows why it's so important to look at the small stuff that businesses usually ignore: emotional connections, employee engagement, employee retention, and community. By focusing on these and other overlooked areas of your business, Brad Sugars and Monte Wyatt give you exceptional tools to build exponential growth."

Craig Handley, CEO of ListenTrust, author of **Hired to Quit, Inspired to Stay**

We thank our families, the ActionCOACH Business Coaching community, our business-owner, CEO, and executive clients, and all of the business world thought leaders we have learned from.

We do what we do because of you.

Pulling

PROFIT$

Out of a Hat

Adding Zeros
to Your Company Isn't Magic

Brad Sugars & Monte Wyatt

Published by Cranberry Press
Distributed by National Book Network

Cover Design: Emily Paige Vincent
Internal Design: Emily Paige Vincent
Editorial Production: Robert J. Hughes
Set In 8-16 Baskerville

Cataloging-in-Publication data for this book is available from the Library of Congress.

ISBN-10:1732049726
ISBN-13:978-1732049727

Cranberry Press is available at a special discount for bulk purchases in the U.S. through its distributor National Book Network (NBN). For more information, please contact the special market department at NBN 15200 NBN Way, Blue Ridge Summit, PA 17214, or call 1-800-462-6420 or email custser@nbnbooks.com

Table of Contents

MARSHALL GOLDSMITH FOREWORD

Building a Happier, More Profitable Business

Business leaders and entrepreneurs often ask me how to define success, and how to build an environment that combines business growth with opportunity for employees to be at their best.

They want to know the best way to ensure exponential growth in their business, with their teams, in their community and in their personal life. Developing as a leader is a difficult endeavor. Today, leaders have many more demands placed on them – and less time to focus on change.

The more that's expected of leaders, the less time leaders have to improve their skills and move their companies forward. They need to know how to efficiently build supportive teams and create an engaged workplace.

Brad Sugars and Monte Wyatt have found a way to do this. They have also developed a system where companies can build explosive growth – and make it look easy. Of course, Brad and Monte know, as leading executive coaches, that mastering anything requires constant attention. Above all, it requires discipline. Here, they will share with you their powerful system for change. They've created what they call the five disciplines that help leaders achieve sustainable, predictable, stable, and consistent success with an emotional connection.

They'll tell you it may look like magic when a company succeeds, but we all know it isn't simply a matter of tricks.

They make a point of focusing on the future – rather than looking for feedback on what has gone wrong. Brad and Monte emphasize a dynamic and expansive way forward, rather than a static look at what happened in the past.

We all realize how much effort goes into making things look easy, and this is true of successful companies. It also requires effort for leaders to instill confidence in their teams and to grow their businesses.

Here, Brad and Monte show you how companies succeed when their leaders have a clear idea of where they want their businesses to be, and a sound strategy for getting there. You'd be surprised at how often business leaders lose track by not having a sense of where they want their businesses to be.

Brad and Monte provide a clear path to success by exploring a multifaceted strategy of decisive action, conscious choices, and disciplined leadership. They show why their five disciplines will lead to continuing success through strategy, business development, people, execution and mission.

Brad and Monte have also developed a new concept that discovers and refines the potential in your business and your team. They show you how to implement new ideas and actions in your enterprise. They believe in

forward-thinking over scarcity – and have found a way to build a business culture that ensures that everyone in the business thinks in terms of growth rather than loss.

They make a point of focusing on the future – rather than looking for feedback on what has gone wrong. Brad and Monte emphasize a dynamic and expansive way forward, rather than a static look at what happened in the past.

What's more, they show how to give employees the motivation that will allow them to grow from within. Creating a great environment is a key factor in building engagement, and everyone has the opportunity to take responsibility for their own lives and to do their best to build engagement – regardless of what the company is doing. Brad and Monte show how to instill in employees a sense of self-ownership, where they take personal responsibility for their own engagement, and thus make a positive contribution to the success of the enterprise.

So, *Pulling Profits Out of a Hat* isn't just a blueprint for corporate growth – but a plan for corporate engagement from the inside out, where employees, managers and business leaders can contribute to creating something truly great and truly successful.

CHAPTER **1**

SOMETHING OUT OF NOTHING
THE MISER'S DREAM

In the middle of an empty stage, a man reaches out and plucks something from mid-air. He holds it up so everyone in the audience can see he's caught a coin that was invisible to them. With a clink, he drops it into a container on stage and then snatches at the air again, grabbing another coin. He repeats this several times; soon the audience can hear a growing number of captured coins rattling and clinking in the container.

The man reaches in and lets the coins slide through his fingers: there are far more in the bucket than anyone might have thought!

He then moves through the audience, discovering coins everywhere he looks — in people's hair, behind their ears. Each time he finds one, he

throws it to his assistant on stage, who catches it in the bucket with another clink.

He returns to the spotlight and pours the coins into another container, much larger than the first … and yet, this more significant bucket overflows with coins that have somehow come from the smaller container. This bucket, almost too heavy to lift, is used to fill a barrel, and it, too, overflows, spilling coins onto the floor. The man holds the now empty bucket up to his assistant's face to catch a cascade of coins from her nose. Wine barrels are scarcely large enough to capture all the wealth flowing on stage. By the end of the illusion, the stage is knee-deep in riches as the magician takes a bow.

This illusion, *The Miser's Dream*, has been performed in one form or another for nearly 150 years. Its roots are practically timeless, for this story of creating gold out of nothing is as old as Midas.

IS IT MAGIC, OR A TRICK?

Obviously, it's a trick. C'mon, if you could produce a stage full of wealth, you wouldn't need to perform. The wonderful thing about this trick, though, is how it delights people to see a fantasy come to life: there's a magical way to make money from nothing.

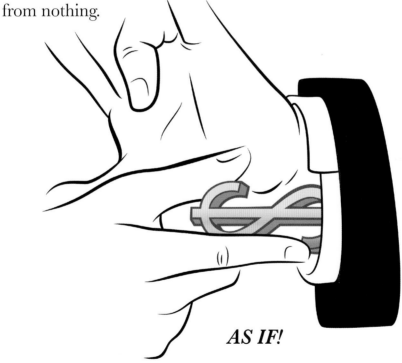

AS IF!

The true magic of *The Miser's Dream* is that no one suspects how much hard work goes into making it look like, well, ***MAGIC***.

There's the magician himself, who has trained for thousands of hours to develop the sleight of hand that makes it look like he can snatch a coin out of midair. There's the army of backstage people and onstage assistants moving like clockwork into the right place at the right time without a single wasted motion so that the audience never notices what is actually happening. And behind the scenes there's a squad of technicians whose skills include hollowing out coins to conceal things inside them.

This team works toward the shared goal of making an audience believe an outrageous idea: it's possible to create something of value from nothing! An entire array of simple effects, like palming a coin, or building boxes with false bottoms, is woven together to unite an audience in a single happy idea: life can be better than it is.

Stage magic is magical because it's *designed* to be. Its point is to create situations where it's easier to believe in mystical occurrences than in all the painstaking work and intricate details that go into the presentation. For example, when a blindfolded magician precisely describes an item belonging to a member of the audience, we're much more likely to label it ESP than to imagine that the magician and his assistant have memorized hundreds of specific phrases to describe any item an audience member is likely to have brought to the theater.

Who works that hard? Effective magicians. And the harder they work behind the scenes, the more successful they become because it's easier to believe in magic than in the labor it takes to make something look effortless. The subtle lesson here is that a person with extraordinary powers has a value that the rest of us don't.

This belief holds true in business, too. Think of Apple's co-founder Steve Jobs, often referred to as a magician who pulled off miracles no one else could accomplish.

WHEN A COMPANY ACHIEVES SOMETHING GROUNDBREAKING, PEOPLE CALL IT MAGIC.

There's a reason people call such feats magic. Magical thinking makes us feel good: Hey, I can't do what Steve Jobs did! He had superpowers no other mortal could hope to have! Let's face it — if Steve Jobs were just a regular guy who worked super hard, the rest of us would have no excuses for failing to achieve the success that we say we want.

We believe Jobs actually was a magician — though not one with supernatural powers. Jobs was a magician like the one in *The Miser's Dream*, whose showmanship concealed a lot of very hard work. And like successful stage magicians who string together a bunch of minor tricks to create major illusions, Jobs very carefully combined the business disciplines found in any company into a single integrated idea designed to astonish audiences. And we're not just talking about the home computer, the iPod, and the iPhone.

Jobs and Apple worked their magic into every factor of their business.

A while ago, we were in the middle of a city on a trip and discovered we had left our iPhone chargers at home. With time before our train, we walked to the Apple store. Arriving before it opened at 10 am, we noticed something important about retail stores in general. Naturally many retailers have them, and they all pretty much have the same basic components, including limited square footage, windows, employees, and stockrooms. After all, how different can you make a store?

Well, this trip caused us to challenge that conventional thinking. Through the Apple store's giant glass doors and windows, we were able to admire its pristine layout of long tables set with row after row of Apple products. That was it. No merchandise on the floor. No sales counters, nothing extraneous. Everything on view was a subtle reminder of the effortlessness that Apple promises its customers.

At 9:45 am, the Apple store wasn't yet open, but there was an Apple employee outside, using an iPad to set up tech appointments for the small crowd of customers who were already waiting. Through the windows of other stores, we could see other employees, on the clock, waiting to open their shops *precisely at 10*.

Once inside Apple, as everyone else went to their tech appointments, an employee immediately greeted us and took us to a wall of accessories. As we talked with him about our trip and favorite places to travel, he ran our credit card through his iPad and the receipt spat out from a hidden printer. There were no counters to come between us and there were no slamming cash register drawers. The effect was that we were having a conversation, not conducting a monetary transaction.

We were on our way in no time; yet, for the rest of the day, our minds kept returning to our Apple experience and how it felt like a magic show, where all the technology, practice, planning, support, and mess of modern commerce was invisible. In its place was a company focused on a single message for its audience: buying technology from Apple is the most human interaction you're likely to have all day.

USE THIS BOOK TO ADD ZEROS TO ACHIEVE EXPONENTIAL GROWTH

This simple trip to an Apple store is a perfect illustration of what this book is about: adding zeros is our term for how it's possible to take what's in front of you and increase its value by adding a zero to it. Consider the times you've gotten a check and wished that there were just one more zero added to the left of the decimal point. Think how much more that check would be worth.

Now think about any aspect of your business and how adding a zero to the end of it makes it that much larger. For example, if you added a zero to the return on investment (ROI) you get from your marketing efforts, and a zero to your average lifetime customer value, those two increases

would multiply each other, and the resulting number would be large. Exponentially large. Now imagine that every aspect of your business — team morale, revenue, margins, customer loyalty, sales, everything — has a zero added to it. The result is ginormous.

In *The Miser's Dream*, a single coin — let's say it was a dollar — becomes two, then nearly a dozen. The magician has added a zero to his first coin: $1 + 0 = 10$. He adds another zero, and now

100 coins fill a bucket. Another zero, and another, and the stage is filled.

Think about how Apple added zeros to its store. An employee already on the clock makes appointments for people so that the moment the doors open, the store wastes no time in making money. Glass doors and windows are as large as possible and clutter is removed to emphasize Apple's streamlined approach to life. Technology is used to increase an employee's ability to engage with a customer. Like a magician finding a coin in midair where the rest of us saw nothing, Apple has taken the ordinary and found value in it. Every one of their investments (windows, employees, inventory control, technology, etc.) has had zeros added to it, increasing its value. More importantly, each zero-enhanced investment multiplies the value of the others, creating exponential growth.

And this is just a single store, just one of the many opportunities Apple has for adding zeros. Is it any wonder they're the largest company in the world?

As you think about your company, ask yourself if you're adding zeros or if you're adding zero.

ADDING ZEROS IS AN OPERATING SYSTEM FOR EXPONENTIAL GROWTH

We like to look at Apple, not just because of its impressive exponential growth but because of the computer connection. We believe that just as we have operating systems on our computers, businesses should have operating systems, too: a series of logical instructions that are coded into the DNA of a company and direct its operations. The business operating system we've created is an exponential growth operating system. It's a process for fast-growth companies — those we call exponential companies — to follow.

Everyone in your company, from CEO to stock clerk, needs to read this book. They all influence your business, and they'll benefit from the clarity of understanding how and why everyone contributes to the magic your company creates for its customers.

We bet you're reading this book because you're a business leader. You know that developing your business is more than just coming up with leads and selling to them.

And that growing your business requires more planning, organizing and executing than anyone thinks … and that includes some of your employees and customers.

Consider the size of the marketplace in which you operate. Does a scarcity mindset — there's barely enough, and I must keep fighting for what I have — prevent you from seeing your potential exponential growth?

LET'S CHANGE THAT!

WHEN YOU UPGRADE TO OUR ADDING ZEROS OPERATING SYSTEM, THERE ARE NO LIMITS.

We believe that with a change of thinking, you and your team could start aiming for exponential increases. Instead of 10% growth, you could be shooting for ten times or a hundred times that much.

This resource guide shows you how to make exponential gains by adding zeros to every aspect of your company. Like *The Miser's Dream*, it's possible to pull vast wealth out of places where it looked like there was nothing. We'll show you that you're surrounded by many more possibilities than you realize and teach you how they can help you achieve sustainable, exponential growth of morale, employee engagement, employee retention, and impact on your community.

This book provides you with a sharp level of awareness, enabling you to see things about your businesses you could not see before (or perhaps were unwilling to acknowledge). And once you've seen your potential for adding zeros, it's a handbook you can regularly use to build and maintain what you need to achieve exponential growth.

DO YOU WANT TO ACHIEVE THESE THINGS? GREAT! WE WANT YOU TO, TOO!

First, in **Part 1**, we describe the 5 Disciplines that will add zeros, and we also detail the 5 Constituencies that every business must satisfy. This will help you understand how they all integrate and depend on each other: you need to develop all of them to create exponential growth.

Second, in **Part 2**, we help you assess your competencies in the 5 Disciplines. Are you serving your constituents as you should? Are you adding zeros? In what areas do you excel? Which areas need help?

In the heart of the book, in **Part 3**, we provide you with specific action steps to help you improve what's working well and to build up what needs help.

And finally, in **Part 4,** we give you the tools you need to put these steps into practice, including guidance on running annual and quarterly strategic thinking and execution planning meetings.

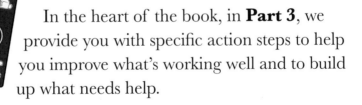

IF YOU'RE ADDING ZERO INSTEAD OF ZEROS, PART 3 WILL BE YOUR HANDBOOK.

This book is about more than just ensuring that your business operates very much in the black. It's about a powerful new and ground-breaking concept that celebrates all the untapped potential in your business and your team. This book will become a trusted resource for implementing new ideas and actions in your enterprise that will wow your constituents … and yourself.

CHALLENGE YOURSELF WITH
SOME QUESTIONS

We're going to challenge your assumptions about how business works, so let's establish a baseline for comparison's sake. Please take the time to write down your answers so you can track your progress as you move forward.

1. How do you define business success?

2. What process do you follow to make business decisions?

3. What's the possible impact of exponential growth on your business, your team, your community, and your personal life?

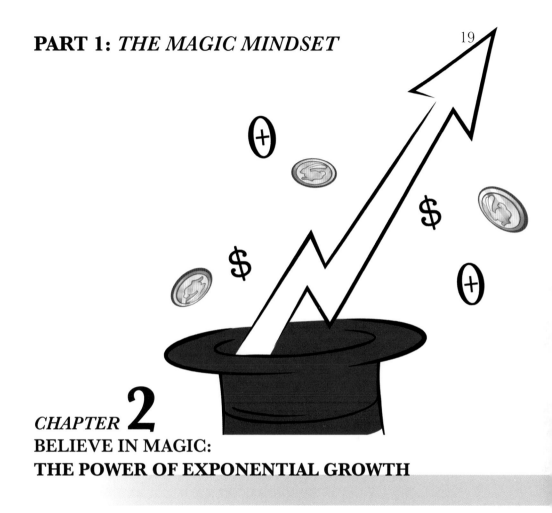

CHAPTER **2**
BELIEVE IN MAGIC:
THE POWER OF EXPONENTIAL GROWTH

*ABUNDANCE IS THE
MINDSET NEEDED TO
ACHIEVE EXPONENTIAL
GROWTH*

As we said, people look at phenomenal business success and call it magic.

MAGIC ISN'T REAL; IT IS REALLY HARD WORK.

To believe in the magic of adding zeros, you first need to accept that it's possible to grow beyond what you are now and that such growth can be and should be exponential.

We know. That can almost seem like believing in magic.

Many of us grew up believing that there's only so much to go around, and if someone else gets a big piece of the pie, that means there's less for us. Most of us learned to base our sense of self-worth on comparisons and competition and to believe that our success results from someone else's failure.

Stephen Covey, in his classic *The 7 Habits of Highly Effective People*, called this attitude the Scarcity Mentality. According to him, people with a Scarcity Mentality have a tough time sharing recognition and credit, power or profit, even with those who help in the production. They also have a hard time being genuinely happy for the success of other people. The Scarcity Mentality is the zero-sum paradigm of life.

A Scarcity Mentality is the belief that resources are always inadequate. Thinking that we must compete for money, opportunity, or recognition means someone must lose, and the fight is one to make sure the loser is someone else. Living and working like this leads to incredible paranoia, fear, and anxiety. No one trusts anyone else and everyone is deathly afraid of making any mistake. Under these conditions, teamwork and innovation suffer and growth of any kind is practically impossible.

As much as we'd like to believe that everyone is optimistic, forward-thinking, and generous, we look around and know that's not true. We know that it's often possible for a forward-thinking company leader to be surrounded by employees with a Scarcity Mentality.

Think about the people who work with you:

- Do they tell people how much they value their contributions?

- Do they see challenges or opportunities?

- Are they worried that someone is getting more than they are?

- Are they glass-half-empty or glass-half-full people?

- Do they acknowledge and appreciate all the positives in their life and work?

- Do they give more than they receive, and do they provide more than just money?

We believe that the greatest danger of this kind of thinking is that it values profit above all else, because gain is the absolute proof that you won and someone else lost.

But wait, you say, profit is the bottom line of a for-profit business, right?

Our answer is: *maybe ...*

We know, that's shocking, but hear us out. We think the concept of a business's profit has overshadowed a more important one: business *success.*

These days, the term profit has taken on darker connotations as society accuses businesses of paying so much attention to profit that they ignore or even endanger workers, customers, and the environment. We believe that in a healthy for-profit business, profit's proper role should be a consistent marker of a company's success and progress. A company should continuously monitor profit as a symptom of its health. Tracking profit this way reminds everybody of the shared goal they're striving for every day.

This use of profit is critical for fixing a common and dangerous problem in business: the "if it ain't broke, don't fix it mentality." If it was good enough for yesterday, why shouldn't it be good for today and tomorrow? This thinking leads to department heads who mechanically repeat the same tasks day in and day out, and don't review, question, or think about how they expect different results. According to some, this is the definition of insanity.

SO, WHERE DOES THIS MENTALITY COME FROM?

As we pointed out earlier, it's leadership. Leaders model behavior for their followers. So, if the boss is happy with the same-old-same-old, well, that ought to be good enough for everyone else. Why should the rank-and-file care about the business more than its leaders?

We've worked with many companies that seem successful, content to set a 30% growth target that they usually define as increased profits, market share, or sales revenues. We believe that a Scarcity Mentality is holding them back from aiming at 30 times that.

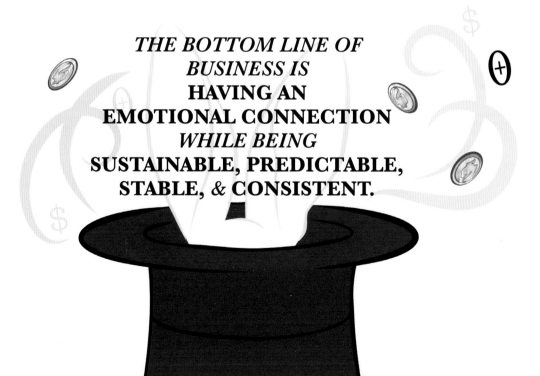

THE BOTTOM LINE OF BUSINESS IS HAVING AN EMOTIONAL CONNECTION WHILE BEING SUSTAINABLE, PREDICTABLE, STABLE, & CONSISTENT.

If all you're thinking about is profit, you're basically thinking that if you don't quickly grab what you can, you'll end up with bupkis. This leads to the unfortunate and shared belief that every business functions like the commodities market for corn, wheat, and soybeans: consumers demand access to a limited supply of product, and whoever finds a way to undercut or better a competitor's prices is the one who wins. It's the win-lose mentality.

The threat in this kind of thinking comes from believing that your business — your bushel of soybeans — is precisely the same as your competitors', so the only way to sell your goods is to have the lowest prices.

But c'mon. Your soybeans are special. There's no comparison to other soybeans, because your soybeans feed more people per pound. Or they taste like chocolate. Or they cure the common cold. Thinking this way, you aren't selling soybeans: you're selling magic beans, and the market rates for soybeans don't apply. You can set your prices to be whatever you want.

If you haven't taken the time or effort to figure out the precise difference between you and your competition, it seems easy to act like a commodity and compete on price because, in the short term, you'll make a profit. But as soon as someone comes along with a magic bean (can we say iPhone?), your shortcut to profit will cripple you (can we say BlackBerry?).

Profit from competing on price is definitely one way to distinguish yourself from the competition: you get a bigger piece of the pie and you win! However, when your customers save money on your low prices they have more to spend, and they do, paying $5 for a latte at Starbucks.

Starbucks didn't achieve exponential growth by competing on price.

Starbucks, Apple, and other companies with exponential growth have worked so hard to add zeros to every aspect of their businesses that the cumulative effects are companies that are magically unique.

Companies that add zeros challenge their specific industry's view of the pie, so let's look at your slice of the pie right now. Regardless of what your business approach is, the products you specialize in, or even which category you belong in, we believe there are four ways to run your business, depending on how you view the pie.

THIS SLICE OF THE PIE IS ALL WE GET

You've seen the guy in the diner, eating alone, his free arm circling his plate, guarding it against anyone taking it. Some people who grew up in large families have the same habit: making sure no one takes their pie.

Some companies operate like that; interestingly, many of them are family businesses. They grow to a certain point and then stop. We call these businesses stationary. They suffer from fear or a lack of knowledge or dreams. They often include sizeable single store businesses, local companies with many outlets in a particular city, and even old, traditional businesses that have become household names.

These businesses don't like change and see no reason to grow, expand, or contract because they're comfortable with their position in the marketplace. Like we said: if it ain't broke, why fix it? But, while they might seem outwardly complacent, they will fight hard to maintain the status quo and their market position, arm wrapped around and guarding their piece of the pie.

Companies like these hit their ceiling and stay there. Some might see that as stability. We only see stagnation.

WE ONLY LIKE ONE KIND OF PIE

At a lot of Thanksgiving dinners with family, there's often a table groaning with every kind of pie you can imagine, ranging from sweet-potato to pecan, to chocolate-coconut-pecan (and worse). And there's someone, usually Uncle Ralph, who won't eat any pie because his favorite — plain ol' apple — isn't there. So, he sits scowling on the couch while everyone else discovers that salted-caramel-peanut-butter-fudge-pie is the future of dessert.

Some terrific companies are wildly innovative and change the way the world thinks or operates. But when they stick with what they like and fail to anticipate or adapt to changing market conditions or their customer's evolving needs, they crash.

BlackBerry once was the epitome of a great technology company: their products defined business communications. But once the smartphone came to market, their taste for a single product line that could only do one thing led to their decline.

IPhones and Android-based smartphones led to increased technological expectations for electronic devices but, like Uncle Ralph, they stayed with what they liked. As a result, they had an 87% drop in stock price and now sit on the couch, scowling at Apple and Google.

These companies hit their ceiling and crash down. Remember: innovation is useful, but constant change is crucial. Always look to the future and over your shoulder.

JUST A BITE, THANKS

There are people who, when served a piece of pie, use their fork to excavate the filling from the crust and eat only that. Or they break off the thick crust from the rim saying they're full and they don't need any more, leaving the rest of the pie untouched and offering it to someone else who knows how to make the most of it.

There are companies like this: taking just enough of the pie to stay in the black each fiscal year even as they mix it up with their competition. They fulfill an essential role in the economy, even if they never set the business world on fire.

Most companies that survive the dangerous years just after startup are operated like this, growing slowly but surely because they can't or don't want to grow at breakneck speed.

This state can last for a long time, and there are a lot of good reasons for it. They might have a conservative business philosophy or lack resources. They could be in the right place, but at the wrong time, or vice versa. They could be ahead of their time, waiting for the world to catch up to them.

These companies grow in small, slow, and steady increments that get them from Point A to Point B and maybe eventually to Point Z … but what about all the points that aren't located on that linear roadmap?

LET'S JUST MAKE THE PIE BIGGER

Most pies are 9-inch diameter circles, cut into six or eight pieces. It's hard to feed a crowd because cutting more slices causes them to fall apart into a mess. Then there's something called slab pie: a massive rectangle of flaky crust and ambrosial filling that can be cut to feed a multitude, each piece as large or small as it needs to be for each person. Make the pie bigger, and everyone can get what they want.

EXCEPTIONAL COMPANIES SEE LIMITS AS OPPORTUNITIES.

Exceptional companies see the limits that hold everyone back and refuse to be confined by them. Consider pre-2007 smartphones, like those from BlackBerry, that had buttons for specific tasks. If a company wanted to change what the smartphone could do, they had to add physical buttons to the phone and convince the public that the new features were worth the cost and hassle of getting a new device.

Then Apple's Steve Jobs got involved. He realized that if physical buttons dictated what a phone could do, they'd limit or even cripple the pace of innovation. His solution was to replace physical buttons with a touch-screen that could be continually adapted to the needs of the phone's software.

This meant that any developer could imagine new uses for the phone and never be challenged by its physical form. Need a new button/function in an app? Design it! The iPhone is infinitely adaptable to every new idea.

As of this writing, the iPhone is just about ten years old, and it has changed the world so much that there's no going back. The smartphone is now an infinitely large slab of pie that includes uses like credit card charging, blood sugar metering, and GPS navigation. Its adaptability means that as soon as someone can think of something to send to you

on your phone, they can …
and then charge you for it. The
pie isn't just larger for people
making phone calls, but for
those who now benefit from the
smartphone economy … and
that's anyone who wants to.

Apple's journey from building
computers in a garage to the
largest technology company
in the world was possible because of their belief in adding
zeros, along with consistent, disciplined, measured, and
mature follow-through. That's what's necessary for taking a
company to the big time.

For a while in the '90s, Apple suffered as it sought to
increase its market share of the PC industry, an industry
where HP, Dell, and all the other PC makers simply lowered
prices, improved performance, or targeted sales in different
channels to steal each other's customers.[1] Apple's then-
leadership believed it needed to be more like HP and Dell,
or even like Microsoft. But merely copying the success of
either the PC makers or Microsoft wouldn't work because
the soybeans Apple was selling were magic (see page
26). Apple didn't need market share; it needed market
expansion. And when Steve Jobs returned and added zeros,
they got it — and how!

1 "Why Apple Failed, Roughly Drafted, October 26, 2006, http://www.roughlydrafted.com/RD/
Q4.06/9FD12E37-8DC7-4AD1-872F-2021BEDE6D96.html

This new phase of the company's history created exponential growth that took it from nearly bankrupt to becoming, in 2018, the first company in history worth more than $1 trillion. Yes, that's trillion with a T.[2]

HOW 'BOUT THEM APPLES?
(SORRY, COULDN'T RESIST).

Apple is now much more than a computer manufacturer or software developer: it is the technology that makes our modern lives possible. Its ability to develop possibilities in every aspect of what it does — as we saw in the store where we bought our iPhone chargers — comes from its belief that everyone has something to contribute to the goal of serving the customer, and that everyone must work together at all times to make that happen.

Apple is obviously the best example of how it's possible to grow exponentially while simultaneously building a long-term, sustainable organization.

2 www.washingtonpost.com/business/economy/apple-is-the-first-1-trillion-company-in-history/2018/08/02/ea3e7a02-9599-11e8-a679-b09212fb69c2_story.html?noredirect=on&utm_term=.9608e580edbc

There are other examples, of course, and all of them have intention, drive, and purpose that create massive excitement in the world of business and the world at large. We'll be referring to many of them as we move forward in this book.

THE LITERAL POWER OF CHANGE...

We know you understand exponential growth, but let's use an example that'll remind you of its incredible power.

Let's say that you start an investment bank account with an opening balance of one cent.

Just a single penny. Yes, we know, what bank would accept that? Indulge us for a moment.

Okay, now, every day for one month, make a deposit that doubles what's in the account. So, on day 1, you add 1¢ for a total of 2¢; day 2, you add 2¢ for a total of 4¢, and so on.

Simple, right? Even silly. And yet, after just two weeks, or 15 days of doing this, your account would hold $163.84. Big whup, you say. But, keep doing it for another 16 days, for a total of 31 days, and now (drum roll, please) your balance is a staggering $10,737,418.24. Yup, nearly eleven million dollars.

THAT'S THE POWER OF EXPONENTIAL GROWTH.

Okay, so you've probably already figured out that to add more pennies to your bank account every day, eleven hundred million pennies must come from somewhere. If you had them to begin with, you wouldn't need the exercise!

SO, WHERE DO THOSE ADDITIONAL PENNIES COME FROM?

Okay, now think about how many times you've seen a penny on the sidewalk and just bypassed it. What's your threshold for picking up small change? Will you pick up a nickel? A dime? Will you pick up a quarter? Do you just dump your coins into the tip jar at the coffee bar to save yourself the trouble of putting it away? A lot of us ignore small change because we don't have time for it. We've already got big bills in our wallets, so we don't sweat the small stuff.

The point we're making is that there are hundreds, thousands, and even millions of small things in your business that you're stepping over because you don't think they could be valuable. But as we've seen, those small things add up. And once momentum gets established, your return will quickly surpass your initial investment.

This should give you an idea as to why most businesses are essentially stagnant: they think they're too big or important to collect the money that's lying at their feet.

Still think you don't have time for the small stuff?

For us, the small stuff that businesses usually ignore is morale, emotional connections, employee engagement, employee retention, and impact on our communities. But when a company commits to exponential growth by making even a modest investment, it can achieve optimal success — as if by magic.

The organizations that have indeed left their mark on the marketplace are those that have grown exponentially; they have multiplied their results, not just added to them, bringing them optimal business success.

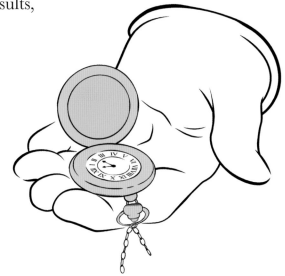

PROFIT IS NOT THE ONLY DEFINITION OF BUSINESS SUCCESS

OPTIMAL BUSINESS SUCCESS SOUNDS GOOD, BUT WHAT DOES IT MEAN?

We can't repeat it enough. Our definition of optimal success is having an emotional connection while being sustainable, predictable, stable, and consistent.

Without a mutually understood definition of business success, a lot of well-meaning people roll up their sleeves, get to work, and never get ahead. If they never define business success for themselves and the company, they'll continue to work at cross-purposes without realizing it.

Desperate for anything that will get them ahead, they grasp at the latest theories, tackle too many ideas, and schedule tasks without fully implementing them. Meanwhile, the shareholders and Board of Directors are breathing down their necks, watching every move, waiting for signs of what they call success. That's an awful lot of wasted effort.

Imagine how quickly this problem could be solved if everyone involved in the enterprise agreed on a definition of success that makes sense for the business, and then developed a plan that had realistic timing and goals to make that happen.

WAIT ... THAT SOUNDS LIKE A TRICK!

Nope. As we've said, not everyone is willing to take the time and effort that exponential growth requires, which is why some people would prefer to think that it's magic instead of hard work and discipline.

The magician in *The Miser's Dream* illusion begins by dexterously manipulating a coin to make it appear from thin air. He then seems to drop it into a bucket, but he invisibly keeps it in his hand to make it look like he's pulled another coin out of the ether. He repeats this action dozens of times in the presentation, after having practiced it for hundreds, if not thousands, of hours to make it unnoticeable. And that's just one of the disciplines he's mastered to create awe in his audience.

Over the years, we've worked with thousands of successful companies that create magic for themselves and their customers, and we've found they all have devoted thousands of hours to the following:

- pursuing the things that will make them succeed;

- reaching a common goal with a high level of excitement and commitment;

- adding value to their clear niche in the marketplace;

- holding a higher purpose than just profit.

Mastering anything requires constant attention to the activity and the skills that it develops or improves. That's the meaning of discipline, and the five disciplines we're about to share with you enable you to perform what will seem like magic. When you and your team have mastered them, they'll be so effortless that the public will never notice them, even if they're right in front of their noses. And just like a huge magic illusion on stage, every one of the five disciplines depends on and is seamlessly integrated with the others so the final result is greater than the sum of the parts.

LET'S GET STARTED!

CHAPTER **3**
MASTER THE MAGIC:
THE FIVE DISCIPLINES OF ADDING ZEROS

There's a reason only dedicated magicians succeed. Learning sleight of hand is frustratingly hard: your fingers don't move correctly, you drop things, that last move never goes right. But when your first audience gasps in awe, you know you're on to something, and you're hooked. Remember when Steve Jobs was on stage and introduced the iPhone in 2007? Yeah, that moment was cool, but it took two-and-a-half years of experiment and failure, and a whole lot of confidence, to even consider making that kind of exponential growth happen.

Growth is about getting to the next stage, and whether that means a coin trick or the iPhone, growing means using muscles you haven't exercised in a while, if at all. Growth is about entering into relationships and going places where you might have no experience. It's a constant state of discomfort, and that's good, because comfort is the death of success. Comfort means taking the easy way out, like competing on price and charging less instead of figuring out what differentiates you from the competition, so you can charge more.

You know what they say: if it were easy, everyone would be doing it, so many people do the easy thing. If you look at it that way, you can see that something that makes you uncomfortable doesn't necessarily mean it's something to avoid. In fact, when you recognize that discomfort is usually just a reaction to something that's unknown, feeling uncomfortable could be a useful way for you to realize that something is not necessarily wrong, it's just new.

For many companies, the process of asking questions and seeking answers about goals for business success is new. It feels uncomfortable. That's especially true when leaders are complacent or asking questions that could reveal problems long ignored.

But that doesn't make it wrong. It makes it necessary.

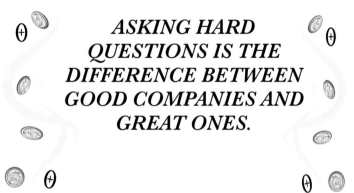

ASKING HARD QUESTIONS IS THE DIFFERENCE BETWEEN GOOD COMPANIES AND GREAT ONES.

For us, this is the difference between the companies that are merely good and those that are great. You may believe that some companies are born great or some have greatness thrust upon them, but we think you achieve greatness with a clear idea of where you want your business to be and a sound strategy for getting it there. This happens through decisive action, conscious choices, and disciplined leadership.

We've identified the five disciplines that help leaders achieve sustainable, predictable, stable, and consistent success with an emotional connection.

They are:

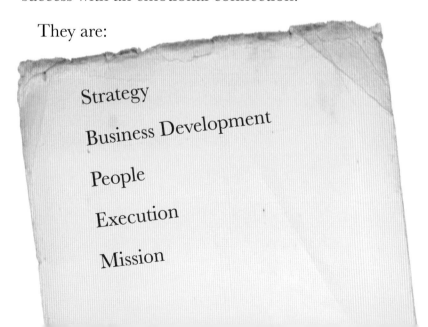

Strategy

Business Development

People

Execution

Mission

They work together with pinpoint precision, much like the performers, equipment, and technicians in *The Miser's Dream.* It might seem like one is more important than another, but the whole thing falls apart when they're out of balance. Mastering these disciplines takes time and dedication, but that's what needs to happen to get the crowd to believe you've created magic.

LET'S LOOK AT
EACH OF THE FIVE
DISCIPLINES AND
HOW THEY MAKE
ADDING
ZEROS
POSSIBLE.

1) The Discipline of Strategy — Sustainability

Your business strategy is your articulation of the way you do business. It consists of two parts: where you want to go (your goals), and the roadmap that gets you there (your plan). Since every company, even those in the same business sphere, is different, every business strategy is different. The important thing is that your plan is appropriately designed to achieve the goals you've set.

Most businesses have built their business models around a product. As a result, they don't have sustainable strategies for their companies: if their product starts to falter in the marketplace, they can't recover (see BlackBerry). These companies believe that the sales strength of their products proves they have successful strategies, but the truth is their strategies are for their products, not for their companies.

STRATEGY IS NOT ABOUT PRODUCTS.

Strategy is about skillful management that attains an end. And that end is more than margin, profit, or revenue — it's sustainability: your business outlasting your competition and, ultimately, you. We call this winning.

Winning, or ensuring sustainability, is one of the prime duties of senior management of any organization. Winning becomes easier when leaders have a clear strategy to guide their decision-making process, because a clear strategy defines how an organization will win.

A clear strategy provides a vibrant picture of what winning looks like for the company, every department and every position.

It identifies **who** is doing **what** to achieve **which** goal by **when**. Without a clear strategy:

- There's no clear direction for the company, so you can't achieve the growth needed for your goals;

- There's no commitment or buy-in from the team, so you can't attract and retain great people;

- There's no business model to drive the organization, so business development becomes a struggle;

- The business is very reactive, so profit is inconsistent or non-existent.

If the team is to continually and consistently implement the company's strategy to succeed, it is critical that everyone can state the company's strategy in a single concise sentence. When the strategy's clear, everyone instantly understands it. When it's a single sentence, it's easy to remember, repeat, and talk about. A concise strategy that's continuously present within the company means that it's first and foremost in everyone's mind, making it easier to make it the focus of everything the company does.

How do you know if your strategy is clear? Every employee should be able to state it in a single sentence. Let's look at a few examples that illustrate this.

Southwest Airlines' single-sentence strategy is *wheels up*, a reminder that the company is only making money when its planes are in the air. Everyone works to keep the fleet on the ground for as short a time as possible. Pilots and attendants work with ground crew to clean planes between flights. Passengers line up with no seat assignments and fill the plane as quickly as getting on a bus. All their planes are Boeing 737s, so crews and staff need to know only one type of aircraft.

The answer to any question is, does it get '*wheels up*'?

The result is a company that's been profitable for over 44 consecutive years — no mean feat in the airline industry. Southwest Airlines has also appeared for 22 straight years on FORTUNE Magazine's list of World's Most Admired Companies, ranking number seven in 2016.

General Electric's single-sentence strategy grew from CEO Jack Welch's goal in 1981 to make GE the most competitive corporation in the world. This became Number One or Number Two in all business categories, or *fix it, close it, or sell it.*

Twenty-five years later, in 2005, this iconic American multinational corporation filed a federal tax return that was 24,000 pages long in a 237-megabyte data file.

IKEA's business strategy in a single sentence is *flat-pack furniture*. IKEA caught the international imagination by providing a wide range of well-designed and functional home furnishings at prices so low everyone can afford them since their *flat-packed furniture* ships so cheaply.

WHAT DOES SUSTAINABILITY MEAN?

You probably noticed that these three companies have a few things in common: they're household names, they've withstood the test of time, and they're all big.

Here's another similarity: they all continue to grow because their business models, while specific to each one's markets and needs, are based on business sustainability. The main reason most businesses aren't very good at creating sustainable strategies is that they don't address each of these four critical areas:

1. Opportunity

2. Leverage

3. Scalability

4. Marketability

In Part 2 of this book, you'll have a chance to evaluate your business strategy and determine how you can add zeros to it. We'll show you how to do that, discipline by discipline, in Part 3.

2) The Discipline of Business Development — Predictability

Wouldn't you do just about anything to be able to predict the future sales, growth rates, or profits of your company, even if they were negative? You'd be able to act to make the most of the opportunities or prevent the calamities. That's why we consider predictability the Holy Grail of business.

Interestingly, you increase predictability when you focus on people instead of profit, because people are creatures of habit. According to *New York Times* reporter Charles Duhigg, about 40% to 45% of what we do every day may feel like a decision, but it's actually habit.[1]

It stands to reason that the more a business focuses on customers (who are creatures of habit) instead of sales, the more likely it is that the business will succeed. If you only focus on sales (profit), you'll lean toward competing on price. But focus on your relationship with your customers, and not only will you learn what led them to buy from you in the first place, you'll also learn what keeps (or could keep) them coming back.

1 "Habits: Why We Do What We Do,"; interviewe with Charles Duhigg, Harvard Business Review, HBR IdeaCast podcast, https://hbr.org/2012/06/habits-why-we-do-what-we-do .

In other words, instead of generating random sales through pricing structures, you'll be adding zeros through your growing base of satisfied customers who like you and want to continue their relationship with you. This creates incredible sustainability for your company.

SUSTAINABILITY SHOULD BE THE PRIMARY CONCERN OF ANY BUSINESS.

Predictability creates sustainability, and predictability comes from understanding the causes of past growth to calculate future exponential growth.

Here are two companies that believe their relationships with people are more important than bottom line profits … and yet, they are very successful.

Hyatt, the iconic American multinational hotel chain, drives revenue by building brand preference.

The company uses sophisticated, quantitative strategic analytics and predictive modeling tools to identify the most profitable customers, enabling it to leverage choice in all facets of marketing. Hyatt's strategy is rooted in a comprehensive understanding of its customer segments, the dynamics of the markets in which it does business, and the effective use of new technologies.

To that end, it focuses attention on the center of its worldwide marketing efforts: the website at hyatt.com. Dedicated teams drive sales traffic, search engine optimization, site management, social media and the all-important Central Booking System, which continually improves upon the customer's booking experience. A crucial part of Hyatt's strategy for building and leveraging relationships with core customers is a specialized loyalty program for meeting planners because the organization's ability to grow top-line revenue focuses on selling conference facilities to the business sector worldwide.

Hyatt's sophisticated mix of modern technology and traditional marketing methods has enabled it to achieve predictability through hyper-focus on the needs of distinct customer segments that its different brands serve.[2]

2 "The Hyatt Difference"; http://hyattdevelopment.com/competitive_strengths/sales_and_marketing.html.

Airbnb is an online marketplace and hospitality service founded in 2008. It's an excellent example of a company that's achieved exponential growth through its mastery of the five disciplines, especially business development and predictability.

Airbnb is a go-between for travelers and hosts, charging hosts a 3% commission to rent their properties as short-term accommodations and charging travelers 6-12%.

Airbnb has over 3 million listings in 65,000 cities spread over 191 countries around the world. By March 2017, the organization had raised more than $3 billion in funding, with the company valued at $31 billion.[3]

As Airbnb owns no infrastructure and therefore has no real estate assets, its entire value derives from the level of trust it creates between hosts and their guests. Airbnb requires that each party completes detailed user profiles so both sides can learn about each other before they meet. Perhaps most important, though, is the public rating system that hosts and guests complete after each stay and Airbnb posts online.

3 "Airbnb just closed a $1 billion round and became profitable in 2016," by Lauren Thomas, CNBC, 9 March 2017; https://www.cnbc.com/2017/03/09/airbnb-closes-1-billion-round-31-billion-valuation-profitable.html.

The Executive Director of Digital Marketing at Fairmont Raffles Hotels International, Michael Innocentin, writing in Hospitality Net, says that Airbnb has given their guests a voice.[4]

Everything Airbnb does starts with its core customers. A comprehensive digital marketing strategy is centered around hosts and guests, leveraging their experiences. Airbnb shares guest photos on social media, runs a blog with local content curated by hosts, and allows hosts and guests to customize its logo. Airbnb encourages users to invite new members to try its services via email, a powerful referral tool, with referrers receiving a $25 travel credit when new members undertake their first trip and a $75 credit when they host for the first time.

Airbnb understands that when guests feel heard, they'll advocate enthusiastically on its behalf, both online and off.

4 Michael Innocentin, "4 Lessons Airbnb's Marketing Strategy Can Teach Hoteliers," by Michael Innocentin, Hospitality Net, September 16, 2016; https://www.hospitalitynet.org/opinion/4078274.html

Understandably, predictability is every marketing person's dream. Ironically, though, we believe that one of the biggest challenges to predictability is that a company's marketing efforts are often inconsistent. To gain that consistency, it's necessary to know and understand the numbers that drive your organization's results. You need to comprehend such things as:

- The return on investment (ROI) you get from your marketing efforts;

- How long it takes to close a typical client;

- Your average client retention;

- The lifetime value of your customers

- How much your customers spend, on average, every time they make a purchase.

It's not enough to know these numbers: you need to use them to educate each person in every department as to how their efforts contribute toward the desired result of exponential growth.

Excellent business development and predictability comes from testing and measuring your numbers in three essential areas:

1. Marketing

2. Sales

3. Customer Service

It's not enough to know these numbers, you need to use them to educate each person in every department as to how their efforts contribute toward the desired result of exponential growth.

Excellent business development and predictability comes from testing and measuring your numbers in three essential areas:

In Part 2 of this book, you'll have a chance to evaluate these areas of your company and the numbers associated with them. In Part 3 of this book, we'll tell you how to understand them and what you can do to improve them.

3) The Discipline of People — Stability

We regard the people who work for your business as being so fundamentally important that we have characterized them as a Discipline in their own right.

A company that lacks stability in this discipline:

- is often distrusted by its staff;

- struggles to find the right people to hire;

- lacks clarity in defining the organization's roles;

- has a team that works to the absolute required minimum.

An organization that is stable in this discipline has:

- high employee morale;

- a very high staff retention rate;

- customers and employees who are treated with the same respect.

So, the first thing to understand is that, as a leader of business, you don't build your business, you develop your people, and they build the business. When CEOs get this right, everything flows from there. The second thing is that exceptional people build excellent companies. The third thing is that the People Discipline is all about the stability of an organization.

The CEO assembles the team that builds the business, so a business's greatest asset is its people. And when leadership regularly and consistently develops those people, they'll have a great company with high employee engagement and retention. Having great people on board leads to a stable business that can weather problems and grow exponentially.

BUSINESSES REFLECT THEIR PEOPLE: THEY GET THE STAFF THEY DESERVE.

When business leaders complain about the poor quality of the labor market these days, saying people aren't as loyal as they used to be, we think they need to examine how many zeros they have in this discipline. Companies that think they have people problems need to examine their practices. Maybe the real challenge is that there's a fundamental flaw in the way the company leads their employees.

Organizations that add zeros to the People discipline are super-attractive to workers and have no difficulty retaining people. When Apple redefined employment as the core of its culture, it added full education reimbursement for workers to its list of employee perks. This created an attraction strategy that appealed to the type of employees it wanted to hire and further differentiated it from its competitors. This means that the people who work for Apple are even more dedicated to the company's culture. They make sure Apple succeeds because it benefits them directly.

> **Marriott International Inc.**, like Apple, understands that people are the foundation of a stable business because without the right people there is no business. And the people at Marriott have built a company with more than 6,500 properties in 127 countries and territories around the world, and revenues of more than $22 billion in the fiscal year 2017.[5]
>
> In 1927, J. Willard Marriott founded his company on this idea: take good care of the associates, and

5 http://www.marriott.com/marriott/aboutmarriott.mi.

they'll take care of the guests. [6] Today, Marriott is an organization that is known as both a great place to work and a great place to stay.

At Marriott, a general manager's average length of service is 25 years, exceeding the industry standard. Of the 361,000 people who work there, some 10,600 have more than 20 years' service. [7]Marriott has also been consistently named one of Fortune's best companies to work for. [8]

Marriott sowed the seeds of its remarkable employee program in 1927, when John ran a root beer stand with his wife, Alice. Once, when one of their three employees didn't show up for work, Mr. and Mrs. Marriott had to pull root beer and wash mugs all day. This experience led them to eventually employ both a doctor and a surgeon to take care of their employees, and to take kids off the street to teach them how to cook. Mr. Marriott promoted from within, turning hourly workers into managers.

The Marriotts still pride themselves on mentoring new employees, whom they hire based in the first instance on their personalities and friendliness.

6 http://www.marriott.com/culture-and-values/core-values.mi.

7 http://fortune.com/2015/03/05/employees-loyalty-marriott/

8 The company was #35 in Fortunes latest ranking. http://fortune.com/best-companies/marriott-international/

Hire friendly, train technically is one of Marriott's slogans, and it's resulted in many Marriott employees now serving as executives who started out pushing housekeeping trolleys, working as waiters, serving as security guards, or working in sales at the entry level.

Today, employees also enjoy flexible scheduling, an assistance-scheme line, healthcare benefits, and travel deals. At the hotels, every shift starts with a 15-minute stand-up meeting that includes stretching exercises, music, and dancing. Who wouldn't want to work there?

Attracting and retaining skilled people is the result of investing in three critical areas:

1. Leadership

2. Talent Development

3. Recruitment

In Part 2 of this book, you'll have a chance to evaluate how well you address these parts of your company. Then, in Part 3, we'll show you how to add zeros to them.

4) The Discipline of Execution — Consistency

Earlier in this book, we faulted businesses that do the same-old-same-old every day.

Now we're going to seemingly contradict ourselves, because we want to make the point that there's a general lack of consistency in businesses today between team members, departments, and divisions, resulting in too much variation in customer interactions. This is extremely problematic for the sustainability of your company, because today's consumer demands reliability from your company.

Consistency provides familiarity and a level of assurance that you have your act together, you're in control, and you're dependable.

Holiday Inn was founded in 1952 by Kemmons Wilson when he was disappointed by the inconsistent roadside accommodations he encountered while

on a family road trip from his home in Memphis, Tennessee, to Washington, D.C. He decided to build his own motel chain that would be remarkably consistent in just about every way. This familiarity helps guests feel comfortable no matter where they are, which means they continue to use Holiday Inns for all their travel.

THE CUSTOMER COMES FIRST. *WITHOUT CUSTOMERS, NOTHING ELSE MATTERS.*

There are only two kinds of customers: new customers and returning customers. If you want the first group to become the second, and you want the second group to continue with you, then everything you do must be customer-focused. These days, finding someone else to supply one's needs is just a Google search away. To retain your customers and grow your base, customers should know what to expect every time they interact with any aspect of your company.

Imagine being the customer of a company that's inconsistent with its customer-facing operations — unfortunately, we've all been there at least once. Such companies are usually plagued with the following maladies:

- Employees don't know what's going on and who's doing what;

- Micro-management;

- Poor communication;

- Lack of follow-through;

- Unclear processes and expectations;

- No clear goals or measures of success;

- Little to no profit.

Now, think about working with a company that's consistent in its operations and exhibits the following characteristics:

- Customers enjoy the same experience as every member of the team;

- Customers enjoy the same experience as every member of the team;

- Everyone does what they say they'll do;

- Employees have responsibility for their roles and are confident in their abilities;

- It's proactive and one step ahead of the competition;

- It's always looking for a better way to do thing things;

- It demonstrates financial confidence and stability;

- It forecasts a positive economic outlook for the months ahead;

- Its processes and efficiencies show constant improvement;

- It practices good management with no micro-management.

Companies that nail execution of their business strategy have researched and perfected what works, and that's how they manage processes while leading people. These businesses guide their people in the consistent execution of fine-tuned processes, every day, in every transaction, by everyone, recognizing that means lots of repetition. Sustainability depends on consistency, which depends on all employees understanding how their actions support the company's goals.

The reason every Southwest Airline crew member picks up trash is that they know their efforts lead to quicker plane turn-around, which increases their on-time record, which increases customer satisfaction, which increases repeat business, which increases growth. High-level, consistent performance like that is the hallmark of great execution.

> Sharing the adverse news of a downturn with his employees set Aziz apart from the typical management practice of only engaging with employees in good times. Being honest and straightforward with his employees paid off: subsequent surveys showed that 90% of Aziz's employees were satisfied with their jobs.

> According to Aziz, employee engagement in times of difficulties and severe economic climate is far more profoundly important now. Employees are willing to give their all when they are well treated and appreciated. And the ability to unlock that potential is a competitive distinction …

it's their decisions, their actions, their attitude that really make the difference. Imagine having 10,000 employees, and each and every one of them wanting to give more. That's really the difference between MGM Grand Hotel and Casino and a company that has its employees just punching the clock and trying to get through the day.[9]

As you can see, great execution comes from good management practices using communication, updates, and progress status reports to ensure that the right things are getting done at the right time.

Once management at the MGM Grand Hotel and Casino began the process of reliably communicating all information, good and bad, to its employees, it added zeros to this facet of its operation while giving them freedom because they knew what to expect.

---

9 Nanette Brynes, "The Issue: Maintaining Employee Engagement," Bloomberg, January 17, 2009.

A company that executes its strategy with consistency is one that has made performing its various processes a habit; there's no need to think about what to do at any given juncture as the next step is reflexive and automatic. When the company as a whole is committed to consistent excellence as a series of habits, it shifts focus from the individual's responsibility and initiative to that of the entire business and its practices built around processes, management, and financials.

Excellent execution of a business strategy depends on developing consistent habits in three critical areas:

1. Processes

2. Management

3. Financial Controls

In Part 2 of this book, you'll have a chance to evaluate how well you address these crucial facets of your company. Then, in Part 3, we'll show you how you can add zeros to them.

5) The Discipline of Mission — Emotional Connection

The Discipline of Mission is not what it sounds like. This discipline is not about mission statements that purportedly explain a company's reason for being, like these:

PayPal: To build the Web's most convenient, secure, cost-effective payment solution.

Intel: Delight our customers, employees and shareholders by relentlessly delivering the platform, and technology advancements that become essential to the way we work and live.

Sony: To be a company that inspires and fulfills your curiosity.

DuPont: To create shareholder and societal value while reducing the environmental footprint along the value chains in which we operate.

Do any of these statements help you understand how these companies achieve their goals? Do any of them help you feel connected to the company? In our opinion, mission statements frequently are esoteric, future-orientated statements filled with feel-good platitudes with which few people will disagree. We believe that mission statements are of little use for a company that wants to add zeros.

A COMPANY DOESN'T NEED A MISSION, IT NEEDS A PURPOSE.

A company should spotlight its impact on the world and answer its employees' question, why do I go to work every day? This is a more profound existentialist question about what the company does in the here-and-now.

For us, the Discipline of Mission is the reason the company does what it does. It describes the whole environment of the company, how it gives back to the community, and why it exists other than just to make money. It outlines a win-win-win situation where the organization grows and employs more people, who then have more money to spend, enabling other businesses to grow. It's about social responsibility.

Social responsibility extends to your employees, your products, and everything your company does. Social responsibility means more than making a positive difference in the lives of our employees and our communities, it involves creating positive change in the world. Doing this adds zeros to your company and everything around you.

We believe that purpose statements built along these lines create strong emotional connections between a company and the people who work and interact with it. E.M. Forster, in Howards End, uses the term "only connect" to remind us of the moral importance of connection between individuals, across the barriers of race, class, and nation.

A company that does not score highly in the Discipline of Mission exhibits the following features:

- employees have jobs rather than careers;

- people tend to show up just on time or late, and leave early;

- high employee turnover;

- low engagement and inadequate involvement with the local community.

A company that fully engages in the Discipline of Mission tends to have employees who:

- have an emotional connection with the company;

- are happy in their jobs and don't regard it as work;

- view their roles as a calling rather than a job;

- are admired in the community.

Chick-fil-A is an American fast food restaurant chain specializing in chicken sandwiches. Headquartered in the Atlanta district of College Park, Georgia, since 1946, it is one of the largest family-owned businesses in America.

The Cathy family, which owns this company of over 2,000 restaurants, operates it based on Southern Baptist beliefs, closing on Sundays, Thanksgiving and Christmas Day. On its website, the company states its philosophy that "everybody's job at Chick-fil-A is to serve: no matter our title or job description, our reason for coming to work is to generously share our time and talents. Whether it's treating customers like friends, or serving our communities like neighbors, we believe kindness is a higher calling."[10]

10 "Everyone's job at Chick-fil-A is to serve," from the corporate website's Giving Philosophy section.
https://www.chick-fil-a.com/About/Giving-Back.

And they practice what they preach. Chick-fil-A's restaurant operators give away food year-round to those who need it most: local shelters and soup kitchens, to first responders and victims after a disaster. And they assist their own employees in achieving their higher education goals. Chick-fil-A employees are encouraged to volunteer on company time to pack meals for hungry children, tend to community gardens or help at food banks.

Chick-fil-A believes that working for them is about more than just serving chicken; it's about having a positive impact in the local community.

S. Truett Cathy, the company's founder, once said, "Nearly every moment of every day we have the opportunity to give something to someone else — our time, our love, our resources. I have always found more joy in giving when I do not expect anything in return.[11]

11 https://www.chick-fil-a.com/About/Giving-Back, December 14, 2017.

The discipline of mission enables people to connect to your company. It's composed of three main ideas that define your company:

1. Core Values

2. Purpose

3. Giving back

In Part 2 of this book, you'll review your mission and the emotional connections it makes possible between your company and your people. In Part 3, we'll show you how to add zeros to your company by creating or rethinking your mission.

In theory, every business has the Five Disciplines already in place and is therefore capable of achieving exponential success by adding zeros to each of them.

HURRAY! LET'S GO!

Uh, not so fast. Unfortunately, when companies put each discipline in a separate silo, treating them as stand-alone components of the organization, there's no compounding effect of exponential growth.

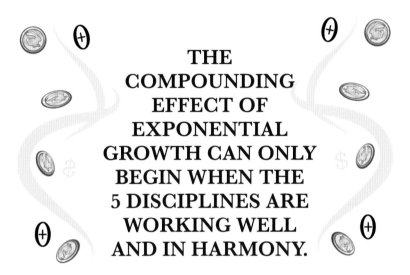

THE COMPOUNDING EFFECT OF EXPONENTIAL GROWTH CAN ONLY BEGIN WHEN THE 5 DISCIPLINES ARE WORKING WELL AND IN HARMONY.

So why are so many businesses stagnant? A company can grow enough to last a while if they have one to three of the disciplines working well. But in our experience, very few organizations recognize who they should be satisfying to grow their business: their key constituents. These are the people who, directly and indirectly, benefit from the company's success.

In a way, your constituents are the audience for whom you're creating the magic of your business, the people who only see the awe-inspiring results of your hard work without realizing how much hard work happens behind the scene to make it possible. As we said before, when a company achieves something groundbreaking, people call it magic. Depending on their background and point of view, they have different belief systems that make it easier to believe in magic than the reality.

In chapter 4, we'll look at how the 5 disciplines add zeros.

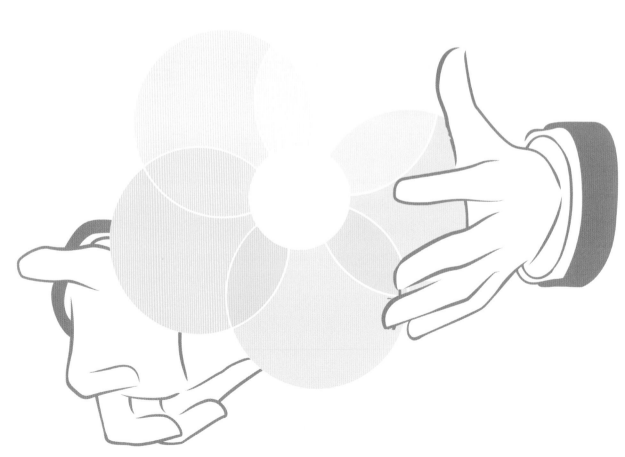

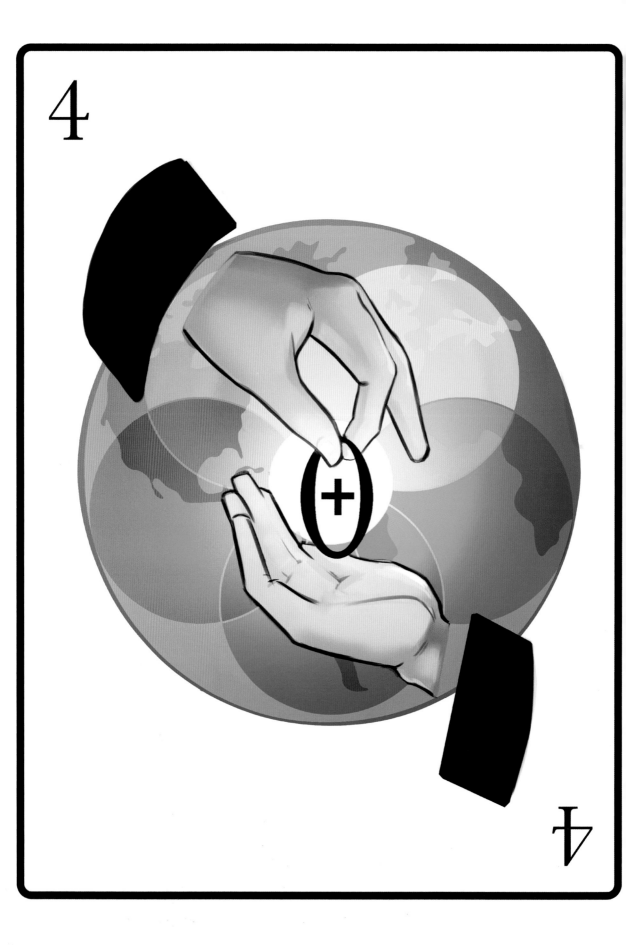

CHAPTER 4
HOW THE 5 DISCIPLINES ADD ZEROS

We believe that every business, regardless of size, can add zeros. That's the point of the 5 Disciplines. As long as you're satisfying your 5 constituent groups by adding zeros to the 5 Disciplines, it doesn't matter if you're a $500,000, or $5 million, or $500 million company with thousands of employees.

Adding zeros to the various disciplines means improving things that can be measured. It's okay to measure things, and you should, because **what gets measured improves.** Once you start measuring something, you unconsciously try to improve it because you're watching it.

You'll see your progress as you add zeros to the various things you measure. If you're not measuring progress in each of the 5 Disciplines, chances are the only thing you're measuring is profit, with all efforts going into improving that number, and only that number.

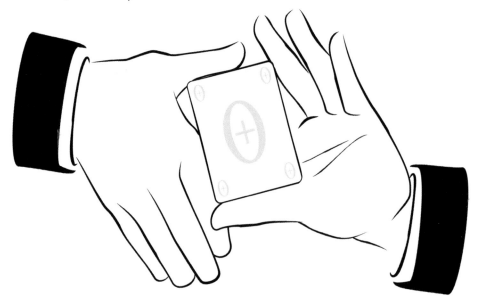

The Discipline of Strategy adds zeros through longevity.

Strategy is about creating momentum for the future, which is seeing where future desire and demand are headed and developing additional product lines to take advantage of those opportunities. It's thinking long term and big picture about what will make you incredible for a long time.

You can't be incredible for a long time if you're only thinking about a single product. BlackBerry, sure, but also think Ford Mustang. If Ford had continued to manufacture the 1965 Mustang forever, it wouldn't be sustainable as a business because it would have only been about that product. Instead, Ford went with a concept that added longevity: it made Mustang about how we feel about ourselves. That gave Ford

big picture and long-term opportunity, leverage, scalability and marketability, the four components of a good strategy.

Ford has been around for over a hundred years because it has thought about filling opportunities in the marketplace that benefit the consumer. You can measure zeros in Strategy by the number of opportunities in the marketplace you're filling. This might mean that growth is slower than some might like, but if you're growing fast, are you really adding zeros to strategy? Growing fast isn't sustainable if you're not satisfying your people, your community, and your team.

The Discipline of Business Development adds zeros through customer acquisition and retention.

Business development is about attracting the right client, servicing the right client, and having high client retention through great customer satisfaction and loyalty.

Successful businesses don't want everyone to be their customer, so they target the specific people who are the best match for the business. This makes it easier to satisfy those customers and makes it likely that they'll be willing to recommend the company to their friends.

Let's say you're losing 20% of your customers every year, and you want to grow your customer base by 10% every year. You'll have to grow 30% every year to reach that 10% growth. But imagine that, instead of losing 20% of your customers every year, you still had every customer you'd ever had since the first day you started business. Now all you must do to grow 10% is get 10% more customers.

Attracting the right customer is marketing and keeping them is customer service. You can measure marketing and sales by number of new customers you gain, and measure customer loyalty by the number of sales to returning customers.

The Discipline of People adds zeros through employee engagement and retention.

The CEO of a 500-person company asked his IT department to complete an important job by a particular date, and their first response was, that can't happen. The CEO pushed them, saying, well, we need this for the customer and their engagement. The IT department told him it would take at least a month longer than the date he indicated, and they refused to engage in a conversation about making it possible.

Now, it would be easy to blame the IT department, but there needs to be an examination of the environment that leads to people saying "we can't" instead of "how can we?"

If your employees say, "I can't do that, that's not my job, they don't pay me enough to do that", you can't necessarily blame them for lack of engagement if you haven't inspired them, trained them, and developed them.

The research tells us that only 20% of employees are fully engaged in their jobs today. That's the result of management that's not engaged.

Engaged management provides the tools that employees need, namely, clear processes that lead to success, the skills for those processes, well-defined metrics for what is expected of them, detailed plans for development and advancement, and, above all, communication.

People don't leave companies; they leave their managers. To employees, the manager is the company because she is what they see and experience. If the manager doesn't satisfy the employees, they aren't engaged with the company,

turn in poor work, and eventually leave. A really great manager practically becomes transparent, enabling employees to see the whole company. A really great manager is also a great leader.

There is a big difference between management and leadership. You manage processes and you lead people.

Making management about competency and productivity, and leadership about **behaviors, focus, and passion.**

A sales team meets every Monday morning to talk about the number of leads they generated in the previous week. To achieve their goals, the company developed solid processes to enable each salesperson to get 10 new leads per week. However, last week, one of the salespeople only came up with two leads. A potential problem. Management asks whether the process was followed. Leadership asks whether something was keeping the salesperson from following the process, exploring their focus and passion- Is something keeping you from following this process? Does this really excite you? Do you understand how to do things? Have you bought into our product and service?

Solving the problem means that management looks at the process separated from the individual's behaviors, while leadership is all about those behaviors. We must have both, and people don't often understand that.

Many companies believe that promoting someone into management means that they're automatically capable of leadership. Many managers think that because they have a management job, they're a leader.

There's a lot of management training out there, but it needs to be balanced with leadership. Otherwise, there will be problems with execution of the company's strategy, because execution is about managing processes.

A person can be a great manager if she follows processes and systems well, but if she has poor people skills, she is not a great leader, and the company will not be successful in adding zeros to the People Discipline.

Adding zeros to People is measured by a lot of things: employee retention, number of outstanding job applicants, number of outstanding new hires, level of morale, number of new skills that employees are trained in, number of employee development plans, job efficiency, and engagement.

You can measure employee engagement by whether people are bringing up solutions, engaging in conversations, interacting with the business, using us instead of you to refer to the company, or completing their work in the expected time frame.

The Discipline of Execution adds zeros through efficiency and effectiveness.

Let's say you only go to a certain restaurant on the nights when your favorite server works because Sally does a great job. When she's not working, you go somewhere else. The restaurant's losing business because it lacks consistent processes that ensure that all servers satisfy customers.

A printing company has three typesetters working the night shift, handling jobs that desperate graphic designers need first thing in the morning to make their deadlines. One of the typesetters, who had experience in missing and making deadlines, provided customers with alternate versions of their copy, especially if he'd caught grammatical errors or problems that would have required waiting for corrections. The designers whose work was done by him were grateful for this extra service, but could never count on getting it every time, as they couldn't request a specific person to set their type.

Creating an organizational process that had all three night-shift typesetters employ this approach added value to the customer at negligible cost because it projected consistency and provided all customers the same value.

Execution is about efficiency, which is not about fast. It's about doing the right things at the right speed to ensure the right quality. This makes quality control a great measure of execution, because errors and mistakes create high costs. If a widget manufacturer must scrap every other widget because it's imperfect, the company's processes and management — its execution — is only operating at 50%.

Adding zeroes to Execution is measured by efficiency and effectiveness. One way to measure efficiency is the speed of service: how long does it take to serve a customer **with the highest quality?** You can also measure efficiency by looking at net sales per square foot, which will tell you about your processes and management of the facility.

THE DISCIPLINE OF MISSION ADDS ZEROS THROUGH EMOTIONAL CONNECTIONS.

A few years ago, we worked with a high-end furniture store to set a Big Hairy Audacious Goal. They decided to be a be 50-50 company, meaning that 50% of their profits would go to supporting their community. They never imagined they'd achieve that goal within 4 years of setting it.

This company's purpose is to help people live life beautifully. Putting their money where their motto is, they gave away two home makeovers worth well over $50,000 for two families who had lost everything, one due to a major fire and another where the father died of cancer. Their attitude is, even though you just went through hell because your house has burnt down, or you just lost your husband or your father, we still want you to live life beautifully. Here's a gift from us to make your home warm, welcoming and inviting.

Now, obviously, not every company can make that kind of commitment to community.

But every company needs to be clear about why they are here on earth.

That is the whole meaning of mission, and it's huge, because profit-crazy businesses have created a monster of a bad rap because they're not helping people.

If we don't support our local communities, what happens? The community has lost faith in us and won't give us tax breaks or promote us as a great place to work. When a company is all about profit, profit, profit and doesn't give back to their community, the community starts to question its relationship with that company- Okay, so they just cut 200 more jobs here and are sending them to another country. Are they really supporting us? Let's re-examine our arrangements with them.

Communities support their local companies with tax breaks and promote them as great places to work. In return, companies have an obligation to give back to the community by adding jobs, paying taxes, providing volunteers for events, and donating resources to community groups.

For example, Principal Financial in Des Moines, Iowa, is a company that took on the mission of helping its local community by investing in that town's waterfront, cleaning it up and contributing to the development of great walking trails so citizens can enjoy where they live. If we expect the government to take care of all our parks and trails and things like that, we're never going to have enough money to maintain and thus enjoy what we have in our communities.

Adding zeros to Mission can be measured by how much money, products, or services are donated to charities like the United Way and other groups, and the number of volunteer hours are contributed to community groups and activities.

WHERE DO YOU NEED TO ADD ZEROS?

You may have recognized some of your company traits in the descriptions of the 5 Disciplines and wondered whether you're doing everything you can with Strategy, Business Development, People, Execution, and Mission to satisfy and benefit the people who make your work possible.

Let's find out in the next chapter, Wowing the Crowds: Satisfying Your Constituents.

CHAPTER **5**
**WOWING THE CROWDS:
SATISFYING YOUR CONSTITUENTS**

MAGIC — THAT IS, STAGE MAGIC — HAS A LOT IN COMMON WITH BUSINESS.

When a magician performs a trick or illusion, the success of the illusion depends on everyone sharing the belief that what they are experiencing is, in fact, real. A magician wows an audience with visions of a better world, one where floods of coins pour from a man's fingertips or a woman floats in mid-air, and because everyone in the room wants to believe those images are possible, everyone is happy.

The magician is pleased to have people agree with him that his version of the world is a better one, and the audience is grateful for a chance to believe in something bigger than themselves.

We think this is true in business, too. After all, what are companies offering if not a better version of the world? Whether it's computer systems or breakfast cereals, companies invite people to imagine a world where their product or service makes life — and the world — that much more problem-free.

Traditional approaches to business only are concerned about getting one group of people to share a belief in a better world: customers. That's why marketing exists.

But we think there are many more people, largely ignored, who deserve to believe in a company's vision of a better world, and they're critical to the success of every company.

A magician must satisfy his audience to succeed. You must satisfy your constituents.

If you break business down, it's pretty simple. It really is.

You must have a vision and a real core purpose and reason for being. You've got to recognize that success is best when it's shared. And you must create a culture and a set of values where people feel like they're part of something larger than themselves. You treat people with great respect.

You exceed the expectations of your people, so they can exceed the expectations of the customer. That's it.

—Howard Schultz, CEO, Starbucks.[1]

1 Here's The Thing, interview, 9/27/16

These days, just staying in business is likely to mean you won't be in business for long. There's too much competition in too many different arenas. To ensure a business's longevity, each discipline must be implemented continuously and consistently so the business works in synchronous harmony. The team performs to their maximum capacity, the production runs are nearly faultless, and the financial situation is healthy.

When the business is not just maintaining each discipline, but adding zeros to each one, typical results include increased revenue and profit, greater customer loyalty, increased employee retention levels and engagement, growing communities, and companies that will last for decades or generations.

However, when just one of the five disciplines is weak, the organization is out of balance, unable to add zeros, and fails to satisfy its constituents. And while it's the nature of business that each discipline will have its ups and downs, that needn't get in the way of pursuing exponential growth. As you'll see in Chapter 6, What's Up Your Sleeve, when there's a problem in the business, it's somewhat easy to identify which discipline is out of whack.

HOW THE DISCIPLINES BENEFIT CONSTITUENT GROUPS

If any organization is to grow, there are five constituents who must be satisfied:

The Company

The Customer

The Team Member

The Stakeholder

The Community

Each of the 5 Disciplines satisfies and benefits two of these constituent groups, as follows:

The Discipline of Strategy satisfies
the Company and the Community;

The Discipline of Business Development satisfies
the Company and the Customer;

The Discipline of People satisfies
the Customer and the Team Member;

The Discipline of Execution satisfies
the Team Member and the Stakeholder;

The Discipline of Mission satisfies
the Community and the Stakeholder.

In turn, each constituent group has a major interest in two of the 5 Disciplines, as follows:

THE COMPANY	
Business Development	Strategy

A Company wants *predictability* and *sustainability*, so the overlap between Business Development and Strategy assures foreseeable, long-term viability for the organization.

> ### THE COMPANY BENEFITS FROM THE DISCIPLINE OF STRATEGY BECAUSE PLANNING ENSURES IT WILL BE AROUND LONG-TERM.

Remember that the company is a constituent on its own and should outlast every person in it. This means seeing and planning for future opportunities that make a company sustainable and long-lived because there are plans for continued revenue and a direction in which to move. The company benefits when people have confidence that it will be around for years to come.

THE COMPANY BENEFITS FROM THE DISCIPLINE OF BUSINESS DEVELOPMENT BECAUSE LONG-TERM PROFIT GROWTH AND PREDICTABILITY MEANS IT WILL BE AROUND FOR A LONG TIME.

Monte took his family to a steakhouse for dinner one weeknight. At 6:30 there was no one else in the place but them. The menu listed several special prices for some of the regular items, and they all decided to have them. But when they ordered, the waiter told them that they'd been given the wrong menus, and the clearly advertised specials were not in effect. For the sake of about $25, the restaurant lost sorely needed repeat customers because they refused to honor a mistake. To no one's surprise, the place closed shortly after. Monte and his family apparently weren't the only ones who felt the place had lost all credibility.

When we get business development right, people know us and where we're going. Not getting it right means we're always trying to get new customers while ignoring the previous ones. Getting 10 new customers a day through our marketing efforts while losing 20 customers a day because our service is terrible is not sustainable: after a while, we'll cycle through every possible client without giving them reasons to come back.

THE CUSTOMER	
People	Business Development

Customers value stability and predictability, so the overlap of People and Business Development pleases them because employee training that rewards professionalism creates expectations of excellent service, leading to repeat business and referrals.

THE CUSTOMER BENEFITS FROM THE DISCIPLINE OF BUSINESS DEVELOPMENT BECAUSE TREATING THEM WELL MAKES THEM HAPPY.

After every transaction at Chick-fil-A, it's standard that employees say, "It's our pleasure to serve you." A small thing, perhaps, but an important one. It honors the human interaction between company and customer. And these days, in a world of mediocre service, this single standard wows the customer. People are wowed by how we talk, how we serve, and how we make them feel.

The Forbes Travel Guide restaurant rating system (formerly the Mobil Guide) awards its first two stars (out of five) for the quality of the food. Stars 3 through 5 represent the level of customer service. When you leave a five-star restaurant, the staff brings you your coat and uses your name to wish you goodbye. Remembering the customer's name, saying please, thank you, sir, and madam are simple, no-cost standards that can quickly add zeros to any business strategy and enable a company to compete on something more than price. When people are not wowed, they focus on price, which limits a company's competitive edge. People will pay more for better service if they see it as a benefit to them. A five-star business strategy is based on what customers consider five-star service, not what the company decides to call five-star service.

The **QuikTrip** convenience store chain might not seem like a 5-star establishment, but employees greet every customer who enters with a simple, Welcome to QuikTrip, even if they're in the middle of another transaction. They let the customer know they've been noticed and brands the QuikTrip experience by making it memorable.

THE CUSTOMER BENEFITS FROM THE DISCIPLINE OF PEOPLE BECAUSE IT MAKES THEM FEEL GOOD.

When a company has the right people in place who have been properly trained and their skills have been developed, and they're enjoying their job, they're building up trust with customers who love how they're being treated. They're going to come back and buy more because the experience made them feel good about themselves.

That could be because the salesperson said they look good in a new suit, or the waitress spoke to them in a personable way. Real human interaction leaves a good impression.

You drop your car off at the dealership at 8:00 in the morning to get something fixed. They say it'll be done at 5:00. So, you show up at 5:00 expecting to drive home, and learn only then that the part never arrived, so it's going to be tomorrow afternoon … maybe.

Not a good feeling.

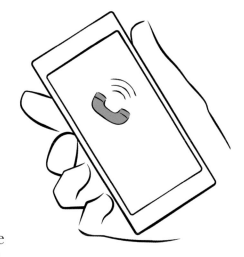

Let's look at a different scenario. After you drop off your car at 8:00, you get a call at 9:30. The dealership tells you, "You know, the problem is bigger than we thought. We won't have the part we need until tomorrow afternoon. Because of the inconvenience, we'll give you a loaner car for two days at no cost if you'd like. We'll pick you up and drop you off."

A fellow human being recognizes that you're going to have a problem and helps you. From now on, you know where you'll be doing business because you were wowed.

When we're wowed, we go back for more of the same. When we're not wowed, we focus on price. It doesn't cost that much to provide wow to the customer, and the minimal investment in empowering employees to wow customers pays off.

THE TEAM MEMBER	
Execution	People

Team Members value consistency and stability, so the overlap of Execution and People pleases them. Reliable and excellent employee training produces high morale and low turnover because people are engaged and cherish their jobs.

> ***THE DISCIPLINE OF PEOPLE BENEFITS TEAM MEMBERS BECAUSE THEY FEEL HEARD AND VALUED.***

There are a lot of organizations where employees don't feel that management listens to them. They continually hear, "We can't do that, that's a stupid idea," instead of, "I love that idea. Let's talk about how we can make that work, and let's look at the upsides and the downsides of that idea, and whether it matches the direction we need to go."

Leadership should respect a team member's input, so they know they've been heard. Coaching a team member to work out for themselves whether their idea is feasible teaches them skills they can employ in the future and rewards them for engaging with the company.

When we're engaged with our jobs, we feel good about ourselves. We're adding value to the company we work for, and we're helping structure the shared future.

Leadership, in essence, is coaching with positive energy, and we get that energy from fun. Fun is important. The more fun we have in our job, the more people want to talk to us, and the more people want to buy from us. Customers can tell when an employee doesn't enjoy their job: there's no wow. Disgruntled employees create disgruntled customers.

We worked with a fast-growing construction company that didn't have a handle on their financials. They had just started understanding their margins, job costing, and all the things that a stable company needs to know. As their attention and energy shifted to numbers, the message the employees felt they were hearing was "it's all about the money now." Without clarification about why the company changed, how it operated, rumors abounded, and resentment grew, endangering customer relationships.

Realizing that the problem stemmed from a lack of clear communication, at the annual team meeting, the CEO said, "Let me show you where the money goes so you know why we can and can't do certain things."

He showed them a stack of $1 bills, saying," Here's one hundred dollars. Let's say this is our revenue for the year."

He counted off a huge number of bills into a pile. "Subcontractors get paid 70% of what we take in every year, so here's $70 gone."

He peeled off 15 singles: "Here's what we pay in wages."

From the much-reduced stack, he made two five-dollar piles: "Here's what we pay in overhead, and here's what goes to taxes."

He held up the remaining five one-dollar bills, fanning them out. "Here's what's left for profit, re-investing in the company, expansion, what have you. We've got low margins in this business. If we all want the company to do more for us, we've got to work together on increasing this pile".

This clear message, delivered by the CEO directly to the team, made them feel heard.

> ### THE DISCIPLINE OF EXECUTION BENEFITS THE TEAM MEMBER BECAUSE EXPECTATIONS ARE CLEAR.

By trusting every member of the team with sensitive financial information, the CEO made them feel valued and raised morale. The reality of five crumpled bills representing the future of the company made everyone realize the importance of making customers feel good.

Many companies give people about 30 minutes of education on how to do their job, without teaching them or coaching them as to what success looks like. Managers just tell the new employee to get to work, and in 30 days, they tell him he's not performing.

Employee: "What do you mean I'm not performing?"

Manager: "Well, you're not meeting our expectations."

Employee: "You never told me your expectations. "

Manager: "Well, you're not moving fast enough."

Employee: "How fast am I supposed to move?"

Manager: "Stop wasting time."

If someone's not performing the way that you want, you ask yourself four questions:

Did we train them on our process?
How can we expect someone to do a job if we didn't teach them?

Is our process correct?
It's possible to teach people a process that's incorrect or inefficient?

Is the employee willing to follow our process?
Does she believe in the validity of the process?

So, what exactly is the process?
Is the process documented, or just in the manager's head?

Execution refers to carrying out the processes that the company has determined will achieve its goals. To execute well means that team members are taught how to perform a process and they understand the realistic results that are expected from that process. When managers make teaching and reinforcing processes a priority, team members know they have the tools to do their jobs, which is a measure of respect. Respect from the company leads to job satisfaction.

THE STAKEHOLDER	
Mission	Execution

Stakeholders are interested in consistency and emotional connection, so the overlap of Mission and Execution is satisfying because dependable performance paired with passion produces a company that does good in the world while producing a profit.

THE DISCIPLINE OF EXECUTION BENEFITS THE STAKEHOLDER BECAUSE ROI INCREASES.

When a company's financial processes are in place and correctly followed, it's making profit, which is of primary concern to investors.

THE DISCIPLINE OF MISSION BENEFITS STAKEHOLDERS BY FINDING BALANCE IN DOING GOOD AND MAKING PROFIT.

Stakeholders want to invest in a company that's figured out how to sustain the community so that earning ROI is possible.

They want to know that they're investing in a company that's doing good things for the world and not dumping nasty chemicals into the river, testing makeup on animals, or other questionable things. Stakeholders want to know that they're investing in something that's good for the world, good for the community, good for the future. It's not just about their pocketbooks.

THE COMMUNITY	
Strategy	Mission

The Community is interested in sustainability and emotional connection, so they're invested in the overlap between Strategy and Mission, making sure the company cares for its employees, does the right thing for the community and is around for a long time to provide the jobs and taxes that make the community possible.

THE DISCIPLINE OF STRATEGY BENEFITS THE COMMUNITY BY SUPPORTING A PLACE WHERE PEOPLE WANT TO LIVE AND RAISE FAMILIES.

The basis of a strategy is long-term thinking that builds a reciprocal relationship between the company and its community: each must ensure that the other will be around to support it. That means communities and companies need to make sure such things as health and education systems attract people who want to live and work there. Think of how long-term strategies have paid off for the communities in which Microsoft, Facebook, and Apple have all built data centers.

THE DISCIPLINE OF MISSION BENEFITS THE COMMUNITY BY PROVIDING RESOURCES FOR SUSTAINABILITY.

When companies invest in community non-profits by providing funds, access, volunteers, and time, they create positive emotional bonds between the community and the organization.

Notice how each discipline satisfies two constituent groups, and each group spans two disciplines, as shown in this diagram:

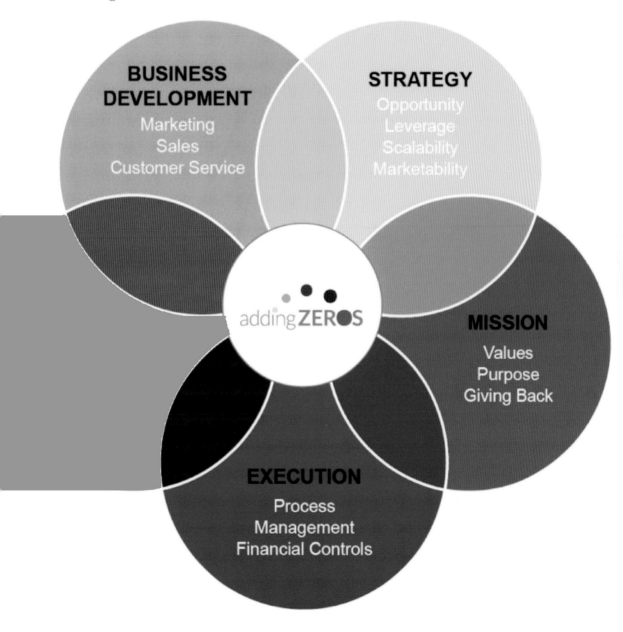

Part 2: Reviewing Your Performance

It's easy enough to understand the concept of sleight of hand: just manipulate a coin so no one sees it until you appear to catch it in midair.

Sure.

Now try doing it. You can read books, watch videos, have someone coach you.

But until you actually put in the hundreds, if not thousands, of hours of practice, it's just theory. Most people won't bother past the initial impulse.

But those who take the time to practice the skills they need to master the discipline then discover that the concepts they've learned can be applied to other ideas in myriad ways, leading to all kinds of new ideas and experiences.

Discipline means concentrating on the end goal, not the steps that get you there. In magic, it can be an illusion that wows the crowds. You can wow the crowds in business, too, with exponential growth.

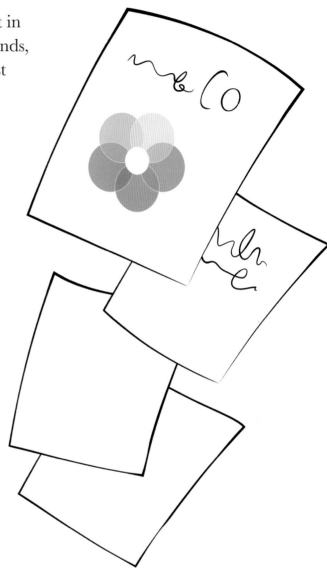

Each one of the concepts we're presenting is a mile deep. They take time and focus to master. That's why we call them Disciplines. They involve learning skills that may be new and hard to grasp, at first. They demand simultaneous focus on the immediate job at hand and future goals.

The 5 Disciplines enable you to think about and plan the balance you need in your organization so that you can satisfy all of your constituents and add the zeros that fuel exponential growth.

Most importantly, like a successful magic show, they require that all involved believe in the value of the reality that is created when everyone believes in the same thing and work together to make it possible.

CHAPTER **6**

**WHAT'S UP YOUR SLEEVE:
TAKE A SELF-ASSESSMENT**

What the Disciplines Reveal About Adding Zeros

Looking at some of the largest companies in the world today reveals how they've had to take stock of their discipline balance and make changes to ensure they were growing in the right direction.

Howard Schultz bought Starbucks in 1987, when it was a small coffeehouse chain. His idea of creating a trendy place where people would pay $4 for a cup of coffee while catching up with friends, holding business meetings, or chilling out with a book or newspaper, took off. In 1989 he had 46 stores, and three years later he had nearly 100 more.

Then it went exponential. In 2007, Starbucks had 15,000 stores in 43 countries, employing over 170,000 employees and generating $9.4 billion in revenue, with reported earnings of $673 million.[1]

However, this explosive growth caused problems: stores reflected a national chain mentality that lacked soul, and customer traffic slowed. Realizing that it was not satisfying its Customer constituent group, who no longer found an atmosphere that was predictable or employees who were engaged, the company addressed the affected disciplines: Business Development and People.

In its 2007 annual report, Schultz wrote, "like some other fast-growing companies, as we rapidly grew and had phenomenal success, we built infrastructure to support that growth which — although necessary —resulted in bureaucracy. We started to lose sight of our focus on the customer and our commitment to continually and creatively enhance the Starbucks Experience.

We will reignite our emotional attachment to our customers and restore their emotional connections with our coffee, brand, partners and stores. And we are building for the long-term — both in ensuring our support functions are focused fully on advancing the customer experience and expanding our exceptional international success story.

1 Starbucks 2008 Annual Report, http://media.corporate -
ir.net/media_files/irol/99/99518/AR2008.pdf.

These — like our commitment to treating our partners with respect and dignity and providing health care and Bean Stock for all of our eligible full and part-time partners — are central to who we are."[2]

By focusing on expansion and profit, Starbucks was adding zeros to just half of the Execution discipline, serving the Stakeholder while ignoring the Team Member. In doing so, it completely ignored the People discipline, and that affected its Customer constituent group. By adding zeros to the Team part of Execution, and to the entire People discipline, Starbucks weathered its sustainability crisis and continued to grow.

As of June 2015, Starbucks had 22,519 stores.

2 Starbucks Annual Report 2007; https://s21.q4cdn.com/369030626/files/doc_financials/2007/2007AR.pdf.

Take a Self-Assessment

Now that you have a more nuanced idea of how the disciplines create an Abundance Mentality and lead to exponential growth, take a detailed assessment of your company to see where you stand regarding the 5 Disciplines.[3] You'll use it as the basis for strategic thinking and execution planning.

Rate your agreement with each of the following statements on a scale of $1 - 5$:

Absolutely = 5   Mostly = 4

Sometimes = 3   Rarely = 2

Never = 1   I don't know = 0

---

3 Adding zeros means you're improving every year. As long as you're not slipping backward, you're making progress. Remember, there are too many components in a business to make it possible to go from zero to 60 in one year. It takes different actions to move the needle. So, every year at the same time, take this assessment to track progression and identify the one or two things that will make the biggest impact on the business.

THE DISCIPLINE OF STRATEGY Rate your agreement with each of the following statements. Absolutely = 5 Mostly = 4 Sometimes = 3 Rarely = 2 Never = 1 I don't know = 0	**Level of Agreement**
1. 100% of our management and our entire team can clearly articulate our strategic direction and plan.	
2. There is absolute clarity about our organizational priorities, and everyone knows how they personally support those priorities.	
3. We spend more time being proactive towards our goals rather than reactive.	
4. We have identified and committed to long term goals and annual goals that support our future.	
5. Our company is positioned for long term sustainability because of the opportunity in the market that we fill.	
6. Our products and services are structured for making a sale once and getting paid long term. (the customer needs to come back again and again)	
7. We have scalability because future sales cost less and are easier to capture.	
8. We know exactly what business we are in.	
9. We are selling what people want to buy and are very marketable to our target audience.	
10. Our team thinks big picture and with a mindset of abundance.	
Total Points for the Discipline of Strategy	

THE DISCIPLINE OF BUSINESS DEVELOPMENT
 	
Rate your agreement with each of the following statements.
    Absolutely = 5   Mostly = 4
    Sometimes = 3   Rarely = 2
        Never = 1   I don't know = 0
	Level of Agreement

1. We have a clear marketing plan to out-perform our competition.	
2. We have a clear sales process and all sales people maximize it.	
3. We consistently provide training and development for all team members who interact with our customers.	
4. We measure customer loyalty and it is consistently improving.	
5. Our target market is absolutely clear, and our marketing efforts attract them.	
6. At a minimum we measure lead generation, conversion rate, and average dollar sale, and strive to improve each one.	
7. We have clear customer service standards and everyone who interacts with customers lives by those standards.	
8. We sell on value and service, and rarely sell on price.	
9. Our business has future predictability because of our consistency in business development.	
10. We are creative and fun in attracting and servicing our customers.	
Total Points for the Discipline of Business Development	

THE DISCIPLINE OF PEOPLE Rate your agreement with each of the following statements. Absolutely = 5 Mostly = 4 Sometimes = 3 Rarely = 2 Never = 1 I don't know = 0	**Level of Agreement**
1. We have a clear process to identify, retain, and/or develop future high potential leaders.	
2. Empowerment and involvement through-out the company is strong and higher than expectations.	
3. We have a clear process for recruitment, hiring, and inducting the best new team members.	
4. All employees have a personal development plan.	
5. We have an effective process for dealing with poor performers.	
6. We have a training curriculum that teaches key leadership skills for our management team.	
7. We have the right leaders in place to be successful over the next five years.	
8. We have a training curriculum that creates great team members at all levels of the organization. (hard and soft skills).	
9. We believe that one great person is more effective than two average team members.	
10. We hire slow and fire fast.	
Total Points for the Discipline of People	

THE DISCIPLINE OF EXECUTION Rate your agreement with each of the following statements. Absolutely = 5 Mostly = 4 Sometimes = 3 Rarely = 2 Never = 1 I don't know = 0	**Level of Agreement**
1. All the company's major processes are written down, trained on, followed and updated periodically for continued improvement.	
2. Every position in every department has Key Performance Indicators to measure progress and success.	
3. We have a visual dashboard of key performance indicators (KPIs) that accurately measure our progress.	
4. We have well-executed communication habits throughout the entire organization.	
5. 100% of our department managers and management team members have a 90-day action plan every quarter.	
6. We are productive vs. active (busy).	
7. We have a culture of peer accountability and follow through. All team members count on each other and trust one another.	
8. We have clear financial goals, budgets, and forecasts for the future that are reviewed weekly.	
9. Every team member understands how they influence cash flow, revenue and profit.	
10. We are constantly improving the actions that create our results. (vs. just focusing on results)	
Total Points for the Discipline of Execution	

THE DISCIPLINE OF MISSION Rate your agreement with each of the following statements. Absolutely = 5 Mostly = 4 Sometimes = 3 Rarely = 2 Never = 1 I don't know = 0	Level of Agreement
1. Our purpose is an emotional connector for our employees and has a clear impact on the world.	
2. Our core values are clearly defined, documented and known by all team members, used to hire, develop, and redeploy our team.	
3. Employee engagement is at an all-time high.	
4. The business direction for the future is clear and motivating to every team member.	
5. We make a positive difference in the lives of our employees, our community and the world we live in.	
6. Our team members are here for a career vs. a job.	
7. Our employee retention is very high (employee turnover is low).	
8. All team members have a sense of pride about our organization in how we represent ourselves and talk with others.	
9. Our organization gives time and financial donations to our community to help those less fortunate.	
10. We have an environment of energy and excitement for the future.	
Total Points for the Discipline of Mission	

Moving Forward with Your Assessment Scores

After you've gone through all the statements, write your score for each Discipline, and then multiply it by 2 to get your percentage scores per discipline.

DISCIPLINE	TOTAL POINTS		% SCORE
Strategy		X 2 =	%
Business Development		X 2 =	%
People		X 2 =	%
Execution		X 2 =	%
Mission		X 2 =	%
Total		÷ 5 then X 2=	%

You'll use these scores to plan priorities for adding zeros to disciplines to achieve exponential growth, so let's look at what your scores indicate, discipline by discipline, and constituent group by constituent group.

Scores for the Discipline of Strategy, serving the *Company* and the *Community*

High Strategy scores indicate:
- long-term sustainability;
- admiration in the community.

Low Strategy scores indicate:
- the company lacks clear direction;
- lack of buy-in or commitment;
- reactionary instead of proactive;
- no clear business model driving success;
- profit is low or non-existent.

Strategy Areas for Change:

   Mindset: abundance and big picture;

   Focus: opportunity, leverage, scalability, and marketability.

Scores for the Discipline of Business Development, serving the *Company* and the *Customer*

High Business Development scores indicate:

- long term predictability;

- strong customer retention;

- you're getting referrals.

Low Business Development scores indicate:

- sales trends resemble a roller coaster;

- selling is based on price;

- the sales team is always chasing new business;

- there is never enough in the pipeline; no idea where the next sale is coming from.

Business Development Areas for Change:

- **Mindset:** fun and creativity;

- **Focus:** marketing, sales, and customer service.

Scores for the Discipline of People, serving the *Customer* and the *Team Member*

High People scores indicate:

- high morale;

- high staff retention;

- future stability within the team.

Low People scores indicate:

- general lack of trust among employees;

- difficulty finding the right people to employ;

- team has poor understanding of their roles;

- team has poor understanding of their responsibilities;

- team does minimum required to keep their jobs.

People Areas for Change:

Mindset: ownership and full participation;

Focus: leadership, talent development, and recruitment.

Scores for the Discipline of Execution, serving the *Team Member* and the *Stakeholder*

High Execution scores indicate:

- high morale;

- high staff retention levels;

- stakeholders experience financial consistency.

Low Execution scores indicate:

- poor communication;

- inconsistencies among employees;

- little or no profit;

- people question whether business is successful.

Execution Areas for Change:

Mindset: habits and routines;

Focus: processes, management and financial controls.

Scores for the Discipline of Mission, serving the *Stakeholder* and the *Community*

High Mission scores indicate:

- admiration from the community;

- stakeholders enjoy an emotional connection.

Low Mission scores indicate:

- employees view work as a job not a career;

- employees show up late or at the last minute;

- employees leave early or exactly on time;

- higher staff turnover than normal;

- poor engagement with the community.

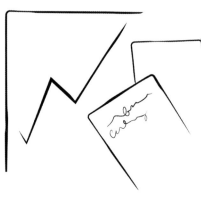

Mission Areas for Change:

Mindset: emotional connection and impact on the world;

Focus: values, purpose and giving back.

Expand your data points.

Of course, this assessment is only your take on the entire situation. To get more data and a better idea of what's really going on with the company, you need to spread this assessment throughout your executive team and your entire organization. We can help you do this. You can take a good assessment test online and distribute it to everybody who needs it. You can find our our online assessment at PullingProfits.com

Develop a course of action

It's tempting to focus on the discipline with the lowest score, but that doesn't necessarily mean it's the area to work on. Work on your most critical issues first, focusing on the issues that, when corrected, will touch 10 other things and cause them to improve. Acting on those things right now will add zeros and make progress toward exponential growth.

The next five chapters are devoted to the 5 Disciplines. Each is examined in detail, paying attention to how it affects its related constituent groups, what action steps can be taken to add zeros, and what metrics can be used to measure progress. As you read through each chapter, reference your assessment so you can see how specific parts of each discipline could improve your performance in that discipline.

PART 3: THE DISCIPLINED APPROACH TO ADDING ZEROS

We said before that for many people a business that achieves exponential growth through adding zeros can seem magical because it's easier to believe that success comes from luck or mysterious forces instead of careful, consistent, and disciplined behaviors.

MAGIC IS A REALITY THAT COULD NOT EXIST IF WE DIDN'T INVEST IN ALL THE NECESSARY DISCIPLINES.

Ultimately, though, it doesn't matter how people believe you've reached your goals as long as you're reaching them. If they want to wait for the fickle finger of fate to tap them on the shoulder while you're slowly but surely adding zeros to every aspect of your business, let them. Some superstitions are impossible to put to rest.

As we discussed in Chapter 3, we believe there are 5 Disciplines you need to master and employ to add zeros. They lead to results that, like stage magic, wow the crowds who refuse to accept that a lot of work and many different steps have led to the joy and wonder they experience. The great news is that, since you're not dependent on mysterious forces for your success, you are always in control of it and can adjust as necessary to continue wowing your audience.

If our system actually was magic, we'd describe each of the 5 Disciplines like this:

1. The Discipline of Strategy is like the Fountain of Youth. No matter how old the company is, its strategy enables it to continually reinvent itself, so that it's sustainable.

2. The Discipline of Business Development functions like a crystal ball. Cues and clues from the past enable predictability, so there's no need to make wild guesses about the future.

3. The Discipline of People references the out-of-control army of hard-working brooms in The Sorcerer's Apprentice section of the Walt Disney film Fantasia because it ensures that when a team of skilled workers has proper leadership instead of being left to its own devices, the company gains stability.

4. The Discipline of Execution is like an incantation or spell, where the right things done in the right order by the right people lead to consistent results —no magical intervention necessary.

5. The Discipline of Mission can be compared to a love potion, because it creates an emotional connection between the company and the people it serves, one that is personally satisfying while amplifying an individual's ability to make the world a better place.

The chapters in the next section of the book break down each of the 5 Disciplines so that you can understand their place in your organization and work to master them, so you can start using them to add zeros. As you learn more about them, remember that they all work interdependently. You can't work on getting just one of them right, they all must be right, and that's an ongoing process repeated quarterly and annually (see Step 4: Putting It Together).

As we said in the last chapter, you may not be able to implement everything all at once, so focus on what changes will add the greatest number of zeros first. The important thing to remember about exponential growth is that these first changes will start to affect other areas in other disciplines. These numerous and multi-level interactions will lead to growth that's so dynamic, you might be tempted to call it magic.

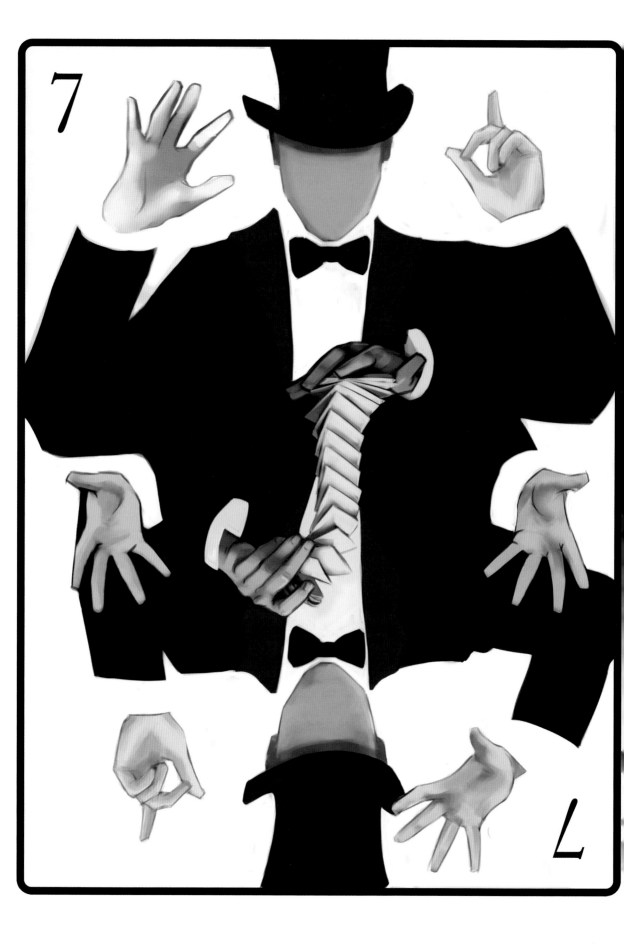

PART 3: *THE DISCIPLINED APPROACH TO ADDING ZEROS*

145

CHAPTER **7**

SUSTAINABILITY: THE FOUNTAIN OF YOUTH

ADDING ZEROS THROUGH THE DISCIPLINE OF STRATEGY

Business history is littered with the bones of companies that grew old and tired and were unable to keep up with new ideas, new generations, and new ways. But if buggy whip manufacturers had been able to bathe in a corporate Fountain of Youth to reinvigorate themselves, they could have embraced the new age of the automobile. It's important to remember that for companies, as for people, eternal life without eternal youth is not a happy fate.

There's no need to search like Ponce de Leon[1] for
something that doesn't exist when the key to a long and
happy life is creating a business strategy that keeps
the organization vital by meeting new challenges and
opportunities with positive energy. Developing a business
strategy is an ongoing process that anticipates what lies
ahead and chooses a direction based on that. Then, when
everyone in a company knows what success looks like,
they can visualize how to help achieve the overall goal.

Everyone can be in the same boat, rowing as hard as
they can, but if they're all rowing in different directions,
the boat goes nowhere. When they're all aimed the
same way, the boat takes off. It's then possible for each
person to expend less energy to keep the boat going, or
everyone can row as hard as before and reach the goal
faster.

When the organization's collective minds develop
their business strategy together, they ensure that all
departments are headed in the same direction, working
with common purpose toward the ultimate goal. This
shared and rewarding activity brings clarity of purpose
and binds the team together, building passion and leading
to job satisfaction.

---

1 Juan Ponce de León (1474 – 1521) was a Spanish explorer and conquistador. He led the first
known European expedition to Florida. A popular myth says that he was searching for the
Fountain of Youth, though no evidence supports this.

This process demands that you are proactive in discussions about the challenges the business faces. Therefore, each of the leaders who take on this challenge needs to cultivate the characteristics of a strategic mindset, as follows:

Thinking futuristically

It's not hard to see how things are today: they're right in front of us. Planning for the future means visualizing what the future holds for your company when you act on your big-picture view of the world.

To think futuristically, do the following:

Be in the present. You can't plan your future without a good grasp on your present. Think about it: how much of your thinking takes place in your 'yesterday' or 'tomorrow'? The Dalai Lama said: "There are only two days in the year that nothing can be done: one is called yesterday and the other is called tomorrow, so today is the right day to love, believe, do and mostly live."

Reject the status quo. Things don't have to remain as they are today; innovation requires change.

Become a generalist. A specialist is easily replaced when their expertise is no longer needed. Generalists don't get lost in the details that can prevent making important connections.

Simplify. Don't over-complicate things.

Strategy fundamentally requires making a wide range of choices, and that can be hard. However, <u>not</u> making a choice is <u>still</u> a choice.

Seeing the big picture

A strategic mindset requires stepping back from the everyday routine to take a panoramic view of the world. A leader needs to recognize the challenges that lie ahead and the opportunities that exist beyond outside one's immediate experience. To see the big picture, do the following:

Step back and detach. Detaching from day-to-day activities enables the executive to focus creative energy on long-term goals and activities.

Keep well informed. By cultivating excellent sources of business intelligence, personal contacts, and business affiliations, the executive can pick up clues about where opportunities lie, where the business needs to head and what pitfalls to avoid.

Ask deep questions. Continually drilling down to a deeper level often uncovers surprising answers that act as catalysts for strategic inspiration. Who is my real customer? Why are they my customer? How do I know they are my real customer?

Collaborate. Working with the entire workforce to develop ideas unlocks creativity, fosters engagement, and energizes the organization.

How to add zeros to Strategy

You can increase sustainability by understanding and using these four components of the Discipline of Strategy:

Opportunity: the demand you aim to fill

Marketability: the likelihood that a product or service will sell

Leverage: using what you have to get more

Scalability: planning the company to ensure natural growth

Let's look at each of these now in detail to see how they enable longevity.

OPPORTUNITY

Opportunity is the demand or market need that your company can fill. It's crucial to explore that demand to determine if there's enough gold in them thar hills to justify the expense of your company trying to find it. If there isn't any gold, brainstorm to find another demand or market need. Don't build a product or company and **then** try to find an opportunity for it.

That's what happened with **Pets.com**. In 1998, they thought their idea of selling pet food and supplies via the internet was so good that researching the market would be a waste of time. Venture capitalists agreed and jumped on board, pumping money into the business; even Amazon signed on. The company engaged in a massive advertising campaign, including a $1.2 million Super Bowl commercial. But sales never met expectations, and in November 2000, Pets.com closed after blowing through $300 million.

Market understanding and research reveals opportunities

Market research could have told Pets.com what solution they could have offered to make a profit or established whether the product or service they wanted to sell was needed or desired in the marketplace.

Reliable market research can come up with all kinds of useful information that answers important questions. Are your target customers already using something like the product you want to market? Is your product or service superior to the opposition's?

Whether you're determining your business's place in the market as an in-house project or you hire a firm, there are three primary forms of market research:

1. **Primary market research** gathers information directly from the market, using interviews, surveys, questionnaires, and focus groups.

2. **Secondary market research** analyzes collected data that has been gathered by you or by others.

3. **Data collection** that is quantitative or qualitative.

Market research can help you understand how and where a product will perform in an existing market. Opportunities can result from a little nudging here, a little sharper focus there.

There are also opportunities that result from new trends and developments that create markets that never before existed. The iPhone is a significant example; here are some others:

In the early 20th century, average Americans citizens didn't brush their teeth regularly. The U.S. Army, during WWI, noted that the state of the nation's teeth due to poor dental hygiene was a security risk. At the same time, legendary advertising executive Claude Hopkins saw an opportunity. A friend wanted him to design an advertising campaign for a new product, **Pepsodent** toothpaste. After researching dentistry and oral hygiene, Hopkins ran a campaign stressing that regular brushing with Pepsodent would remove the ugly film of plaque that makes teeth dull and discolored, and create a bright, sparkling smile. Five years later, Pepsodent was one of the best-known products in the world, the leader in a new market and the new habit of daily tooth-brushing.

The ubiquitous presence of cell phones among consumers, the network that ties them together, and the cell-towers that provide global positioning presented an opportunity to the founders of **Uber,** who realized that they could create a system that would instantly locate anyone with a phone and dispatch a nearby car to them. The components had been in place for a while before Uber connected the dots.

Like Uber, Airbnb saw the potential of a network of empty rooms in different countries that they could make available to travelers. They connected supply with demand in a manner only made possible by the internet, which they saw as an opportunity.

An explosion in makers of **frozen yogurt** — Yogurtland, Menchie's, Pinkberry, Sweet Frog, You Say When Yogurt, Yogen Früz, FroyoWorld, Red Mango, and Orange Leaf, among others — resulted when health trends depressed the market for ice cream, creating an opening — opportunity — for a healthy option for ice cream lovers.

> ## *WE ALL EXPECT OPPORTUNITY TO KNOCK ON OUR DOORS, ANNOUNCE ITS PRESENCE, AND WAIT FOR US TO ANSWER.*
>
> ### *IT DOESN'T WORK THAT WAY.*

Opportunity is created, not discovered. Whether through careful research and reading of the numbers, or matching trends and technological developments, an opportunity is not something to wait for. If you're looking for your lucky chance or big break, wait no longer. Do your homework and take advantage of the openings you find before someone else does.

MARKETABILITY

Marketability isn't a binary condition. You can sell anything if you can find the right buyer for it; the right buyer being defined as the person willing to buy your specific product at your specified price at your specified time.

Adjusting some of those variables can make something more or less marketable; that is, easier or harder to sell at those terms.

As such, marketability is a spectrum that gauges ease:

- the ease of efficiently and affordably accessing the right audience;

- the right audience's ease of understanding what you're saying;

- the ease with which your solution solves the right audience's problem or need.

You can evaluate a product's marketability by determining your company's ease in achieving these things together with your ease and speed of expansion, and whether you can support the level of growth implied by your expected sales.

Apple Computer's AppleCare is all about ease. Seth Godin experienced this firsthand when he called Apple after his PowerBook broke down. Just two hours after the call, an Airborne Express truck pulled up and took his Mac away in a cardboard shipping box custom-made to fit PowerBooks. It was returned 48 hours later, working flawlessly.[2]

Apple efficiently reaches an audience for its AppleCare service program by targeting Macintosh users, like Godin, who instantly understand the product and how it can quickly solve their problems. They're willing to pay for a service that means they don't even have to leave the house. As a result, AppleCare's marketability is practically off the charts.

2 Seth Godin, Godin, Seth . Purple Cow; Transform Your Business by Being Remarkable. (PenguinPenguin Books, 2005), p. , p. 129.

LEVERAGE

Leverage is making what you have, go further. It's like a strategically placed crowbar that enables you to push on one end to move something substantial at the other end. Understanding where to apply leverage can help you move mountains.

Your product's value — what the consumer feels they're getting in exchange for their money — acts like leverage. The better the product's worth, the more consumers want it and the more advantage you have. Increasing the product's value increases your leverage, which enables you to gain a positive outcome, like additional revenue and improved margins.

IT IS MUCH EASIER TO PUT EXISTING RESOURCES TO BETTER USE THAN TO DEVELOP RESOURCES WHERE THEY DO NOT EXIST.

—GEORGE SOROS [3]

3 George Soros (2007). "Age of Fallibility: Consequences of the War on Terror,", Public Affairs, pp.182., PublicAffairs

Simply put, leverage is the advantage that exists when a person or entity has the upper hand. They may have achieved this position from a variety of means including a more significant knowledge or experience base, exclusivity in a particular market, lower product pricing, better service options, or even excellent personal relationships -- with emphasis on the word personal.

Leverage is about using what you already have and using it to get more. In sales, chasing down new leads and hunting for new business is the most obvious way to boost sales. In fact, most salespeople can get so caught up in looking for new customers that they ignore their most significant asset — their existing clients. Sometimes, the single best way to make more sales is to leverage your relationships with people you've already done business with, keeping in touch with them and fostering relationships. You already know those customers and what they need: pushing on the end of that knowledge crowbar can move something else into place.

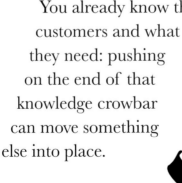

> *YOUR WORKFORCE IS*
> *YOUR MOST*
> *VALUABLE ASSET.*
> *THE KNOWLEDGE*
> *AND SKILLS THEY*
> *HAVE REPRESENT THE*
> *FUEL THAT DRIVES*
> *THE ENGINE OF*
> *BUSINESS, AND YOU*
> *CAN LEVERAGE THAT*
> *KNOWLEDGE.*
> *— HARVEY MACKAY* [4]

Leverage enables you to do more with less, maximizing the value of what you already have. For example, if you've already created a single product, you could leverage your investment in making that product (patterns, processes, software, whatever) into selling it multiple times. Think of software or franchise systems: after the first iteration, you can duplicate success. After you've done something the first time, leverage produces future income or business from with less time and effort.

---

4 This is a widely cited quote from Harvey Mackay, the bestselling business writer, but we cannot locate its source. Mackay has said similar things in other books, such as The Mackay MBA of Selling in the Real World, 2001, Portfolio/Penguin, 2001. Mackay wrote, "My philosophy is this: Employee loyalty begins with employers. Employees should know that if they do the job they were hired to do … you will support them. You will take an interest in their career advancement and give them the tools they need to perform effectively. In return, you as the employer can expect that your workforce is prepared to give its best effort every day…. There is a common goal that can be reached only if everyone pulls together for the good of all." From Chapter 4, "Loyalty in Little Things Is Huge."

Every business should have precise systems in place internally to encourage the creation and use of leverage in the areas of money, people, processes, and technology to benefit marketing, sales, fulfillment, invoicing, etc.

Netflix leveraged digital streaming to provide millions of movies to customers without needing to invest physical copies of them. It costs Microsoft next to nothing to sell copies of Windows after it financed its development. In 1964, American Airlines replaced the old paper-and-pencil with the SABRE electronic ticketing system it developed for its use and then licensed it to every other airline.

SCALABILITY

Scalability is your ability to maintain or improve profit margins while your sales volume increases. If you're scalable, you won't have trouble growing. However, if your systems can't handle the additional workload, you may find that you're going broke even as you're breaking sales records. For example, if you have a long lead-time between ordering

from suppliers and their deliveries, you may find that you can't fill incoming orders and may need to pay higher costs to other sources to fill demand, lowering or even eliminating your profits.

On the other hand, a business with excellent scalability can quickly generate new leads to source new customers even while maintaining the same level of excellent customer service that led to the increase in activity. In fact, a business that can scale up its operation can not only handle the increased workload but take advantage of it.

A business that can scale up can automate specific processes to take advantage of more significant numbers, think about an automated assembly line. The first sale carries the highest costs, everything that the company has invested in the product is counting on that first sale. Additional sales lower the per unit cost to the point where it can become negligible.

Scaling up production means there needs to be similar growth in your customer base making sure there are enough core consumers who need the solution you're offering. This increase could come from expanding markets to other locales to find customers, or franchising or licensing agreements.

Familiarity with the day-to-day challenges in a business can make it difficult to see how that company can scale up. An insider might say, we're too busy dealing with the business we have and how can we possibly take on more? Someone who was looking on from the outside, with a different perspective, might be able to suggest how an investment in growth (a new employee, a new piece of machinery) would make current processes more efficient while increasing capacity for new business. If you can't see the forest for the trees, invite someone else to take a look.

Building the company bigger doesn't have to be something you do yourself. Scalability can come from leveraging your success so that others pay you for following in your footsteps.

Franchising

Franchising is a method for expanding a business and distributing goods and services through a contract relationship. Franchisors specify the products and services offered by their franchisees and provide them with an operating system, brand, and support.

A franchisor's brand is its most valuable asset. Based on what they know, consumers decide which brand to patronize and how often. They trust the brand to meet their expectations, and the franchisor and the other franchisees in the system must meet them.

Great franchisors provide systems, tools, and support so their franchisees can live up to the system's brand standards and ensure customer satisfaction. The franchisor does not manage and operate the locations that serve consumers their products and services on a day-to-day basis. Serving the consumer is the role and responsibility of the franchisee.

Some of the more common services that franchisors provide to franchisees include:

- a recognized brand name;

- site selection and site development assistance;

- training for franchisees and their management teams;

- research and development of new products and services;

- headquarters and field support;

- initial and continuing marketing and advertising.

Licensing

The licensing business model has far fewer restrictions and limitations than franchising. It's commonly used for the sale of products when a company has invented or developed a product or process and then protected it by a patent, copyright, or trademark. Another party seeks access to the product or process to advance their own business. An owner may also grant a license when someone else wants to use an established business name; the licensor receives a royalty as compensation and retains ownership of the intellectual property.

This model has some significant advantages for the licensor, including the following:

- the licensor doesn't have to finance the commercialization of the innovations;

- the innovation gets to market more quickly;

- the innovation can reach a broader market;

- the licensor avoids execution-related risks;

- terms in the licensing agreement protect the licensor from product-related liability.

THE MAGIC OF ADDING ZEROS THROUGH STRATEGY

Throughout the centuries, people have wished to live forever and magicians have been happy to help, inventing all kinds of magical spells, potions, and amulets. Even today, people who live over 100 years are regarded as having miraculous powers for outliving the average lifetime. This fascination with lifespan can be problematic for businesses: it's hard to imagine a company outlasting the people who run them now. Be that as it may, a company can achieve immortality.

Thinking long term and big picture about what will make you incredible for a long-time results in longevity that has real benefits for your constituents.

STRATEGY	
Company
long-term continuity	Community
tax revenue long-term employment

The Company gets long-term continuity, and the Community gets tax revenue and long-term employment for its residents.

As you saw in this chapter, the Discipline of Strategy increases sustainability:

- market understanding and research identifies **opportunities;**

- **marketability** — the variable(s) can be adjusted to sell a specific product at a specific price at a specific time;

- **leverage** gets more out of what you already have; and

- **scalability** strategically exploits current and future capacity.

While we may not live forever, we can ensure that the companies we've built will long continue to make the world a better place to live and work.

CHAPTER **8**

PREDICTABILITY: THE CRYSTAL BALL

ADDING ZEROS THROUGH THE DISCIPLINE OF BUSINESS DEVELOPMENT

A fortune teller with a crystal ball doesn't actually predict the future: instead, she reads subtle cues from her clients: how they wear their clothing, the questions they ask, even the rate of their breathing as she surreptitiously probes what they're really looking to hear. A fortune teller is an expert in using what she learns about a customer's past to tell him what he wants in his future. No crystal balls or tarot cards necessary.

Understanding your customers' past behavior is key if you want to grow exponentially, meaning business development must be viewed in a new light: predictability. Whether you're a CEO, line manager, or department head, your ultimate goal should be predicting your business's future based on proven marketing techniques, a fabulous sales process, and second-to-none customer service.

We create predictability by testing and measuring for a period of time and then analyzing the resulting data. This tells us whether the actions we're taking are giving us the results we need. When we know what action produces which result, we have reasonable certainty about how to have the future we want. Achieving exponential success doesn't require a crystal ball.

How to add zeros to Business Development

You can increase predictability by maximizing these three components of the Discipline of Business Development:

- Marketing
- Sales
- Customer Service

Let's look at each of these now in detail to see how they enable exponential sales growth.

MARKETING

Predictability is every marketer's dream: knowing with a high degree of certainty where to find the next customer and when and what they'll buy. Unfortunately, inconsistent and haphazard marketing efforts prevent this, mainly because many people don't know there's a difference between advertising and marketing. They think marketing is advertising. It isn't.

Marketing consists of two principal activities: education and communication. According to Dan Kennedy's book, The Ultimate Marketing Plan, marketing is getting the right message to the right people via the right media and methods. With this in mind, realize that while advertising — placing ads — both educates and communicates, there are other parts of marketing that do that, too, which is why advertising is just one part of the larger concept of marketing. [1]

As such, everyone associated with a company — investors, team members, owners — shares responsibility for its marketing. Each person should have a copy of the organization's marketing plan and be so familiar with it they can state what the organization does, how it differs from the competition, and who the core customers are.

---

1 Dan S. Kennedy, The Ultimate Marketing Plan, (Adams Media Corporation, 2000), p., p. vii.

The Marketing Plan

A marketing plan is a comprehensive document describing what a business will do to accomplish specific objectives within a specified period. It outlines how, when, and how often the company will get its message in front of its core customers.

A great marketing plan:

- is documented;
- shows a return on investment (ROI) for the dollars spent;
- describes the core customer(s) in detail;
- explains how the company solves the core customer's needs, answering why us?
- outlines how the company will get its message in front of the core customer;
- is action-oriented;
- includes a timeline of action;
- highlights why the company differs from the competition (brand promise);
- includes measurable outcomes for gauging success;
- contains budgets for all activities.

The marketing plan sets out what consumers need to know about the business and how the company will communicate that information to them and everyone in the organization.

The Purpose of the Marketing Plan

The entire organization must understand the purpose of the marketing plan: generating a direct response to produce a return on investment (ROI) or brand improvement, for which there is no measurable ROI.

Understanding the marketing plan is critical because marketing is a massive investment for the company to make. If a campaign is designed to raise brand awareness, everyone must understand that there is no direct expectation that the campaign will directly pay for itself. Direct response campaigns drive sales because they get consumers to buy as a result of encountering the promotional plan.

The Components of Marketing

- Branding

- Pricing

- Lead Generation

- Direct Response

- Product Management

Let's examine each of these in detail.

Branding

Branding involves far more than a company's logo: it's everything the company does. Branding extends down to the smallest details that make you stand out and differentiate you from your competition. And you decide what those features will be.

Why should people buy from you instead of another company down the road, across the country, or online? Because you have a clear understanding of your customer's needs, wants, and desires, and what you're promising them.

The promises you make to your customers are your brand. According to Duane Knapp, a recognized authority on building authentic brands and a pioneer in the field of brand science, a brand promise is the new currency for success.[2]

---

2 Duane Knapp, The Brand Promise, (McGraw-Hill Education, 2008).

Brand success, he says, rests on the following three principles:

1. Providing a unique experience with products or services that enhance your customers' lives.

2. Inspiring employee partnership, passion, and support.

3. Creating the perception of exceptional value and distinctive benefits and delivering on your promise.

Pricing

Pricing is a precise process, not a gut feeling.

Your pricing should reflect the confidence and benefit you bring to your customer. Customers are willing to pay more for excellent service and perceived value, so it makes sense to provide that value

at an optimal price, creatively educating and communicating to your customers that you are offering much more than a perceived commodity. If you and your customers think you're offering a product or service that's the same as everyone else's, you'll live and die by price.

For that reason, we don't recommend sending proposals that encourage clients to look at your price instead of your benefit to them. If you're asked for bids or estimates, we suggest using a Client Action Plan (CAP) to show the value that you provide and how your approach uniquely solves their problem. A CAP leads off by describing the benefit to the customer, and then explains your process, your timing, your ROI, and the timing of specific actions and results.

Lead Generation

Generating leads is the process of collecting lots of data about potential consumers and analyzing it to find potential sales. It is possibly the single most crucial part of business: without a constant stream of new customers who are first identified by a lead generation process, companies would need to rely on repeat business alone without much hope of attracting new business, and that is not a recipe for longevity.

Technology — most specifically, the internet and social media — has rendered many traditional strategies — classified advertising, radio campaigns, host-beneficiary relationships, and referral programs — obsolete. Generating leads today requires fresh approaches to reach new markets, sales channels,

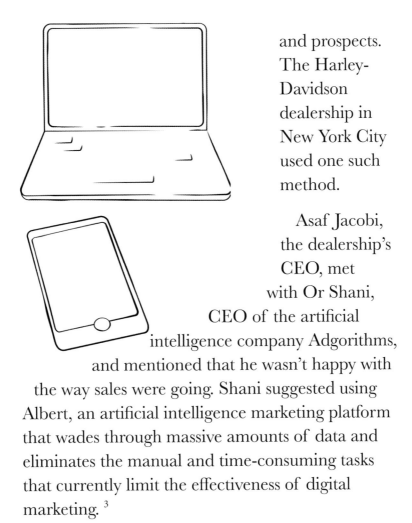

and prospects. The Harley-Davidson dealership in New York City used one such method.

Asaf Jacobi, the dealership's CEO, met with Or Shani, CEO of the artificial intelligence company Adgorithms, and mentioned that he wasn't happy with the way sales were going. Shani suggested using Albert, an artificial intelligence marketing platform that wades through massive amounts of data and eliminates the manual and time-consuming tasks that currently limit the effectiveness of digital marketing. [3]

The first weekend that Jacobi used Albert, he sold 15 motorcycles, doubling his sales. He quickly increased his qualified leads from 1 per day to 40. After three months, website views increased by 566% and leads increased by 2930%.[4]

---

3 https://albert.ai/about/
4 "Harley Davidson NYC hits all time high with Albert" https://albert.ai/harley-davidson-nyc/ .

Jacobi had to hire six new employees just to handle the demand. Analyzing the dealership's key performance indicators (KPIs), business logic, and minimal past customer performance data, Albert's artificial intelligence discovered trending behavior at lightning speed in real time. It used continuously incoming information to identify new audiences and recognize top-performing creative and messaging combinations, prioritizing them across all digital channels.

The Consumer-Oriented Model of Lead Generation

This model is a far cry from the 60-year old traditional marketing approach known as the 4 Ps. Also known as the producer-oriented model, the 4 Ps mandate a focus on Product, Price, Promotion, and Place, pushing your message into the world.

Since modern buyers can learn almost everything about your business online, the 4 Ps are an incredibly old-fashioned way of marketing. Instead, you need to focus on attracting consumers to you and your information. Craig Bloem, Founder, and CEO of FreeLogoServices.com, recommends a consumer-oriented model based on four fundamental questions:

1. *Who are you talking to?* Get to know your core consumers. Learn their needs and understand their concerns. Study how they consume information and where they search for solutions.

2. *What are you saying?* Perform a competitive analysis to learn how you stack up against your competition and then tailor your message. Make yourself different in a way that's sustainable.

3. *Where do you say it?* Choose your channels and map your resources accordingly. Focus on the channels your prospects use.

4. *How do you know it works?* Set growth targets and track your results.

Your Core Consumer is the model for leads

As you can see, the consumer - oriented model means you must know who you want to attract - your core consumer, who's the person most likely to buy your product or service. There needs to be enough of them to buy in the quantity required for optimal profit. [5]

Before you can set about developing new leads for your business, it's important to know who you want to attract - the core customer for your product. Your core customer is the person most likely to buy your product or service in the quantity required for optimal profit.[6]

The person most likely to buy your stuff is the person who needs it, they're buying a solution to a problem. Not the person who wants it but needs it. It's important to understand their need because they might not even know they had this need until they hear about what you have to offer. You are providing what Robert Bloom calls a tangible and emotional customer benefit.[7] Your product or service meets a need that the customer may not even be aware of until they learn about you. Did anyone know they needed a smartphone until they first saw one?

---

5 Robert Bloom, The Inside Advantage: The Strategy that Unlocks the Hidden Growth in Your Business. (McGraw-Hill Education), 2007).
6 Robert Bloom, The Inside Advantage: The Strategy that Unlocks the Hidden Growth in Your Business. (McGraw-Hill Education, 2007. Ibid
7 Robert Bloom, "The Common Sense of Business Growth" http://gicoaches.com/wp- content/uploads/downloads/2012/05/Bob-Bloom-Common-Sense-ATL-May-2012.pdf.

Every company should define their core customer in two sentences: 25 words that include their demographics, psychographics, wants, and needs. Since it's entirely probable that you'll have different core customers for each of your products, groups of products, or services, you'll need separate definitions for each of them. These ensure that everyone in the organization knows who you're trying to attract.

You may already describe your core customer using demographics, the dry facts such as age, marital status, gender, race, ethnic origin, education, household size, and occupation. We think you should also focus on psychographics, which is information like buying behaviors, hobbies, spending habits, and values. Demographics explain who your buyer is, while psychographics explain why they buy.

Psychographics help identify leads

When you understand your core consumer's demographics and psychographics, you can reach them effectively. Combine both sets of data to create your core customer's buyer persona: a detailed description of who they are and what motivates them to buy.[8]

Here's some fundamental demographic information about a nutritional counselor's core customer:

- Female

- Aged 45-65

- Married, with children

- Dealing with issues of weight gain, diabetes, lack of energy or hormonal imbalance

- Household income $100K+

Demographics alone are not enough to create a marketing plan for reaching customers like this. While you might understand her needs related to nutrition, you have no idea where to find her or what moves her to action.

---

8 "What Are Psychographics?"by Maggie Butler, HubSpot; https://blog.hubspot.com/marketing/what-are-psychographics-faqs-ht.

Psychographics gives you so much more insight into what's important to her, your core customer:

- Concerned with health and appearance;

- Wants a healthy lifestyle, but doesn't have much time;

- Enjoys going online in the evenings, big fan of Pinterest;

- Tends to favor quality over economy;

- Finds fulfilment in her career and family;

- Values time with a small group of friends.

She's spending her free time on Pinterest, so stop spending money on Facebook, newspaper, and magazine ads that offer deep discounts. Instead, use Pinterest to share time-saving household and nutrition tips or ideas for fun things to do with family and friends. Post stories about how your nutritional counseling service has worked for others, improving health without a considerable time commitment.

Then watch what gets re-pinned and analyze what that tells you about her. If she loved the smiley-face veggie platters for after-school snacks, offer more ways to help keep her kids eating well. If the girl's night out inspirational quote went over well, suggest things to do to have fun with friends.

Knowing more about her hobbies and interests will help you when you need to choose a prize for your next contest, what to blog about, and what sorts of images to use in your next ad. Before you know it, you'll have more qualified leads than you thought possible!

Psychographics are indispensable in today's marketing environment. Here are two methods of collecting them.

Interview Existing Clients

Next time you talk to your current best client, ask her to tell you a little more about herself. When you ask the right questions, you can find out what she does for fun, whether she's a bargain-hunter, what motivates her, and what her personal goals are.

What was your weekend like? What good movies have you seen lately? No? You're more of an online entertainment fan? Have you found any great holiday deals or made any New Year's resolutions?

If your relationship allows it, be direct and tell her exactly why you're asking. If not, consider talking to friends who are like your ideal client.

If you want a larger sample, send out a customer survey that's open and honest about telling your clients that you want to understand better what they care about. Most people are more than happy to share.

Website Analytics

A more behind-the-scenes kind of investigation involves analyzing your existing website content and previous special offers. What has moved people to click, call, or buy? These actions reveal people's real motivations. They may not think of themselves as bargain-hunters, but if a discount code worked, you know the truth.

Direct Response

Since direct response plans are meant to inspire consumers to buy a product immediately, they should follow the classic AIDA formula: Attention, Interest, Desire, and Action. [9]

- **Grab Attention** through a message, image, emotion, or all three.

- **Pique Interest** by relating to a core customer and their specific needs.

- **Create Desire** with a vision of life once your solution has solved their need.

- **Give a Call to Action** to tell them what to do, such as make a purchase or call a number.

Product Management

Every product or service should have:

- clear market positioning or messaging;

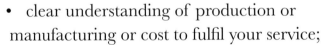

- clear understanding of production or manufacturing or cost to fulfil your service;

- a future direction or long-term view of where that product is going.

---

9 The AIDA model describes the steps or stages that occur from the time when a consumer first becomes aware of a product or brand through to when the consumer tries or buys a product. The AIDA model was developed in the late 19th century and has been modified and expanded to reflect new advertising and communications platforms. It remains one of th most popular so-called hierarchy models of marketing. https://en.wikipedia.org/wiki/AIDA_(marketing)

Defining and managing your products or services helps the team and the business with clear direction. Product management is a proactive and intentional approach to guiding your offerings, product, and services.

SALES

We all love to buy, but nobody wants to be "sold." Scott Edinger, the author of The Hidden Leader, says the widespread resistance to being sold something stems from an antiquated idea that selling is pushing people to buy something they don't want, don't need, or can't afford. But it's not. Selling is moving somebody else to action, according to Edinger, and that is part of professional life.[10]

We agree. Our definition of sales is professionally helping others to buy. That means everyone in a company should be moving someone else to action every day, whether through creating exceptional products or services or by educating prospective customers as to the benefits of the company's offerings. The whole organization is involved in selling, not just the sales department. That's important to remember because, without sales, there is no business.

---

10 Rebecca Knight, "How to Improve Your Sales Skills, Even If You're Not a Salesperson" by Rebecca Knight, Harvard Business Review, May 22, 2017; https://hbr.org/2017/05/how-to-improve-your-sales-skills-even-if-youre-not-a-salesperson

An Educated Consumer Is Your Best Customer

People want to know the benefits of a product or service, so they can decide whether it addresses their need, which makes educating the prospect a significant part of the sales process. This process is a two-way means of offering the customer various options to explore as they gauge the product's suitability.

One of the benefits of engaging in an education process like this is that it builds strong, long-lasting business relationships.

Education benefits the business because people prefer doing business with those whom they like, respect, and trust.

The Sales Playbook

An efficient sales process doesn't just educate a potential customer about products and services. A proper sales process first guides **salespeople** to determine if a prospective buyer represents the company's core customer. Second, the sales process gauges whether the potential customer will be happy with their purchase. This process leads to high conversion rates, avoiding problems caused by selling to the wrong audience, not understanding buyers' needs, or attempting to sell them something they don't want.

A reliable sales process also helps salespeople monitor what's happening in the process by having them confirm each step in the sales process with customers to keep them involved and informed and to provide a sense of urgency to help close the sale. The goal is to reduce or eliminate risk by satisfying concerns before they become unresolved issues that block a sale.

For this reason, it's necessary to ensure that everyone in the sales department has a copy of the company's sales playbook. It's a reference manual that codifies the sales process, so it's predictable, repeatable, and scalable.

A powerful sales playbook contains the following sections:

1. Annual Goals or Key Performance Indicators needed for success:

- **history of results and past measurements;**
- **number of appointments;**
- **conversion rate;**
- **average dollar sale;**
- **total revenue;**
- **margin;**
- **number of total customers needed;**
- **number of new and repeat customers.**

2. Expectations of salespeople and others involved in the sales process

    a) Skills/behaviors

    b) Weekly/monthly expectations for

      i) activity

       ii) productivity

       iii) individual KPIs

       iv) individual goals or measurements of success

3. Essential characteristics of core customers or customer segments

    a) their needs/wants

    b) their demographics

    c) their psychographics

4. Products, services, pricing, and terms

    a) pieces of the marketing plan to share where you fit in the market

    b) comparisons to competition

    c) clear positioning

5. Tools and resources to assist in gaining and managing sales

 a) Customer Relationship Management (CRM) technology

 b) brochures/1 pagers/white papers;

 c) internal and external incentives, promotions, or sales programs.

6. Outline of the sales process: the steps you use to guide a prospect in professionally helping them make a decision.

7. Proven, open-ended questions that reveal the prospect's needs and wants

 a) Examples of actions, touchpoints, and steps to initiate, build and deepen relationships

 b) Options and activities to ask for the order

8. Common objections that we receive and how to handle them

    a) listing of 6-8 typical objections

    b) methods and/or scripts for resolving these situations without the need to escalate them

9. Steps to take after confirming the sale

    a) How to place the order

    b) How to onboard a client or customer

    c) How to fulfill the order or service

    d) Flowchart showing who does what

10. Ways to show gratitude and thank a client for being a customer.

Now that we have a customer, it's time to examine customer service.

CUSTOMER SERVICE

Excellent customer service is a mindset that places the needs of the customer above your own <u>at all times.</u> An attitude of gratitude reminds everyone that the company appreciates the customer's business. A mindset centered on appreciation is positive and proactive, making it easy for people to do business with you.

As Jeffrey Gitomer says in his *Little Gold Book of Yes Attitude*, "every business winner has one thing in common: a YES! Attitude that's powerful enough to help them achieve the impossible! When you've got a YES! Attitude, you assume everything will start with YES! … and you'll find a way to YES! even when the first, second, and third answer you hear is NO![11]

This mindset will empower employees and increase job satisfaction. It supports a positive frame of mind at work, so people leave for home feeling right about their day. Continually thinking about how to put the needs of others above one's own makes

---

11 Jeffrey Gitomer, Jeffrey Gitomer's Little Gold Book of Yes! Attitude, , by Jeffrey Gitomer,(2018 Sound Wisdom; 2018), https://www.gitomer.com/product/little-gold-book-of-yes-attitude/ .

people into better decision makers who consistently treat their customers with respect. And a smile!

Train your team

Some people say that the only people who have to worry about customer service are those who work in the Complaints Department.

Uh… no.

Everyone in your company is responsible for customer service because they all interact with representatives of each Constituent Group (customer, team member, stakeholder, community, company). Even if they don't directly communicate with customers, they might encounter suppliers, distributors, and other members of their team, members of the community: you never know. And treating everyone with gratitude and putting their needs above one's own makes this standard of behavior a company habit.

No matter who a customer or constituent encounters, their experience should be consistent, meaning that providing excellent customer service should be automatic for everyone in the company.

Each employee at every level should be clear about and

have practice in your customer treatment expectations. There should be a short list, in clear, concise, and understandable language, of expectations and standards, not rules or policies. It could be as simple as this three-step process:

- Aim for consistency.

- Make it easy for customers to buy.

- Introduce the WOW factor by surpassing every expectation.

Another good statement of standards comes from the highly relationship-focused K. Renee women's clothing boutique in West Des Moines, Iowa. Jeff Schulz, the owner, says, "We believe that the lifeblood of our business is the relationships we've forged with our customers and our team members.[12]

The company achieves this with their customer service standards, defined by the acronym RELI:

- **R**elate

- **E**ngage

- **L**ess me/More them

- **I**nspire

Remember: people will pay more for exceptional service. The difference between a 2-star hotel and a 5-star comes down to the level of service, with a price tag to match.

12 K. Renee is a clothing and home décor store in west Des Moines, Iowa. It caters to a general consumer public as well as to professionals in interior design and real estate. www.krenee.com

Use the right numbers

When making decisions that will affect their future, companies with exponential growth use facts, not speculation. They know the figures that drive their business, how long it takes to close a typical client, the average client retention rate, return on investment (ROI) from marketing efforts; your customers' lifetime value, and how much they spend on each purchase.

Sustainable businesses know these numbers and use them to identify the actions that create results. They do this by creating Key Performance Indicators (KPIs) for each department and each position in that area. The KPIs are used to measure progress, comparing today's results with yesterday's and with the projections for tomorrow. As a result, every member of the team understands how their work contributes to a winning company with consistent leads, a consistent conversion rate, and repeat customers.

Measuring the right numbers for predictability with KPIs

An organization creates natural links between its goals and corresponding

Key Performance Indicators (KPIs). High-level KPIs may focus on the overall performance of the company, while low-level KPIs may focus on processes in the sales or marketing departments, or in a call center. Some common KPIs include measures of foot traffic year-over-year or month-over-month (sales); number of repeat customers compared to new customers; and various quality metrics. The specific numbers a company tracks are dictated by its current goals and may change over time as the business evolves and sets new performance measures.

Some KPIs are lagging indicators and simply show results from the past. Financial metrics are classic examples of these types of measures. They show the results of past programs and campaigns. They may not have value in predicting future performance but can help managers assess whether they're on track to meet the organization's goals by measuring employees' success in achieving their objectives. In customer service, this can include such leading indicators as lifetime value, customer loyalty, and Net Promoter Scores. Examples of lagging indicators for customer service would be financial reports, previous sales numbers, and the number of total customers in the past.

Other KPIs are leading indicators, which provide guidance on future results. For example, lead generation from campaigns, conversion rates, average dollar sale, customer satisfaction, and client retention can all predict the future.

The focus is on having the right balance of both leading and lagging indicators and improving them.

Some key challenges include:

- Unclear strategy and company goals, so measures focus only on lagging indicators, such as financial outcomes;.

- Too much reliance on financial indicators, providing an imbalanced and incomplete view of the company's health;

- Lack of KPIs as focal points when departments manage their resources for reaching goals;

- Compensation tied to key performance indicator

targets, which introduces conflicts of interest and bias;

- A definition of what success looks like for the individual, the department and the company as identifying appropriate leading indicators can be difficult without this understanding.

A healthy process for identifying and implementing key performance indicators requires regularly revisiting and revising the measures.

Number of transactions

A critical KPI is whether the number of transactions a customer makes is above or below the company's baseline number. If this KPI decreases, strategies for success include:

Making customers feel extra special. Use their name as much as possible and learn and remember their interests. Find out about their family and do something for them.

Under promising and over delivering. Do a little more than the customer expects. If you say the product will be in stock on Wednesday, get it in on Tuesday, and call them on Monday to let them know the good news. This isn't as easy as it sounds but keeping something small in reserve can produce surprising results. There is a catch, however, the more you deliver, the more the customer expects.

Delivering consistently and reliably. All it takes to lose a reliable customer is a single bad experience. You are only as good as your last encounter, so don't become complacent.

Keeping in regular contact. Endeavor to contact with all your clients at intervals that make sense for your business, but at least every three months. Your business is the last thing on their minds, so make your correspondence memorable. A personalized postcard is more special than an email; a special offer can inspire a call or a visit.

Informing customers of your entire range. A customer looking for a specific solution may not be aware of everything you offer. Introducing them to even a single additional product or service could produce tremendous results. If they trust your company, they'll be more inclined to do further business with you for other products and services. After all, they're probably buying what they need from someone else already.

Increasing your range. As you discover what your customers need, keep accessories or complements to existing products in stock. Advertise and alert your customers as to what you offer.

Making sure you always have stock. Nothing is more annoying for a customer who needs something than to be told that it's out of stock, especially items that comprise your core business. When they buy it elsewhere, they might just stay with their new supplier.

Offering closed-door sales. Create exclusive after-hours sales that are only open to existing customers. Provide excellent bargains with drinks and refreshments.

Net Promoter Score

A broader measure of predictability is customer loyalty. People prefer to buy from those they know, like, and trust. When a business knows their customers are loyal, they can be sure they'll get valuable repeat business. And since word-of-mouth (now called Social Proof, in the digital age) is the best form of advertising, when loyal customers tell others about you, you're likely to get new customers in addition to repeat sales.

The Net Promoter Score (NPS)[13] is a system that rates loyalty by determining how many customers are Promoters, Detractors, or Passives.

13 Net Promoter or Net Promoter Score (NPS) is a management tool that can be used to gauge the loyalty of a firm's customer relationships. It was developed by Fred Reichheld, Bain & Company, and Satmetrix. Reichheld introduced it in his 2003 Harvard Business Review article "One Number You Need to Grow." https://en.wikipedia.org/wiki/Net_Promoter.

Promoters are loyal customers who say they'll recommend the company to their family and friends.

Detractors are those who are unlikely to recommend the company and may even speak against it. Passives are satisfied in general but could just as well do business with someone else.

A business, to determine its NPS, asks its customers a simple question: On a scale of 1 to 10, how likely are you to recommend this company to your family and friends?

Nines and tens denote Promoters and add a point to the score (1). Sevens and eights are Passives and add no points (0). Sixes and below indicate Detractors and receive a negative point (-1). Add the points together, and divide the result by the total number responses, giving the Net Promoter Score as a percentage of promoters.

A perfect 100% means every single customer would promote the company without reservation. An NPS close to zero indicates that customers don't care either way. Negative numbers show that work needs to be done to ensure that customers spread the word about your company.

To follow up on scores below 6, design a survey asking for information about what could be improved. All NPS surveys should be as simple as two questions, one of which should be the open-ended, what can we improve? This provides a fairly accurate map for addressing shortfalls and making the business more predictable.

According to loyalty experts Fred Reichheld and Rob Markey, efficient Net Promoter Systems have three requirements:

- a simple and reliable metric for gauging how well you have earned your customers' loyalty;

- operational processes to support action and learning by front-line employees;

- sustained commitment from leadership who model inspirational behaviors.

This is all nicely summed up by Jeffrey Gitomer's rather long title for his book: *Customer Satisfaction Is Worthless, Customer Loyalty Is Priceless: How to Make Customers Love You, Keep Them Coming Back and Tell Everyone They Know.*[14]

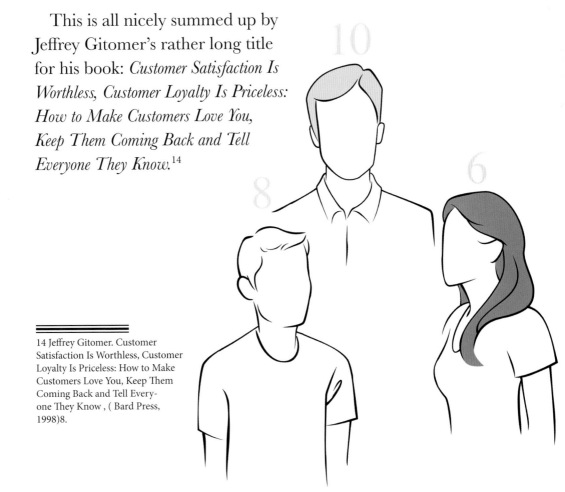

14 Jeffrey Gitomer. Customer Satisfaction Is Worthless, Customer Loyalty Is Priceless: How to Make Customers Love You, Keep Them Coming Back and Tell Everyone They Know , (Bard Press, 1998)8.

THE MAGIC OF ADDING ZEROS THROUGH BUSINESS DEVELOPMENT

Tell people you can predict the future and they immediately start thinking of fortune tellers in veils and turbans before crossing the street to avoid you. Show your customers that you can anticipate their needs because you know what's coming and they'll run across the street to see you.

As you've seen in this chapter, foreseeing your future exponential success isn't magic, it's using past performance to calculate future growth. It's steady, painstaking work that, when done well, seems like magic because no one wants to believe you've worked that hard. That work is necessary to build the predictability that benefits your constituents:

BUSINESS DEVELOPMENT	
Customer *develops and rewards consumer loyalty*	**Company** *long-term sustainability*

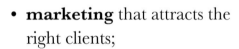

the Customer by developing and rewarding consumer loyalty and benefits the Company by promising long-term sustainability.

As you saw in this chapter, the Discipline of Business Development increases sales growth through:

- **marketing** that attracts the right clients;

- **sales** that professionally help the client to buy;

- **customer service** that retains clients by rewarding loyalty.

While we may not live forever, we can ensure that our company will long continue to make the world a better place to live and work.

CHAPTER **9**
STABILITY: THE SORCERER'S APPRENTICE

ADDING ZEROS THROUGH THE DISCIPLINE OF PEOPLE

In the classic story of Sorcerer's Apprentice[1], an old magician departs his workshop, leaving his apprentice with chores to perform. Tired of fetching water by pail to fill a cauldron, the apprentice puts on his master's magic hat and enchants a broom to do the work for him – using powers in which he is not yet fully trained. Satisfied that the work is being done, he takes a nap.

---

1 Most people today are familiar with this tale from the 1940 Walt Disney movie Fantasia, which dramatizes the 1897 symphonic poem of the same title by French composer Paul Dukas. Dukas based his work on the poem by the German poet Johann Wolfgang von Goethe, which first appeared in 1797. https://en.wikipedia.org/wiki/The_Sorcerer%27s_Apprentice.

The apprentice awakes to the floor awash with water because the broom has continued its job even after the cauldron is full. He finds that he cannot stop the broom because he doesn't know how. In desperation, he splits the broom in two with an axe – but each of the pieces becomes a whole new broom that takes up a pail and continues fetching water, now at twice the speed. He continues to chop away, with every piece becoming a new water-fetching broom that contributes to the flood. Finally, the sorcerer comes back and with a wave of his hands returns everything to normal, leaving his apprentice to clean up … with a broom.

Clearly, there are going to be problems when someone thinks that all he must do to lead the team is wear the leader's hat. A simple change in leadership can wreak havoc when a smoothly working team no longer has someone to balance its systems. Treating a team like a gang of mindless robots instead of persons can have disastrous consequences.

A team of people who feel valued and positive about performing the processes that are designed and fine-tuned for the company's success gives a company stability.

How to add zeros to People

You can increase stability by focusing on these three components of the Discipline of People:

- Leadership

- Talent Development

- Recruitment

Let's look at each of these now in detail to see how they increase team engagement.

LEADERSHIP

Leadership and management are not the same things. We manage processes. We lead people. Leadership creates passionate and focused people. In his *7 Habits of Highly Effective People*, Stephen Covey says management is climbing the ladder of success efficiently, while leadership determines whether the ladder is leaning against the right wall.[2]

Victor or Victim: the point of decision

Leading is all about understanding ourselves and others and how we respond or react in the moment when decisions are made. That moment or point of decision separates two kinds of people: victors and victims. Victors play above the point of decision, and victims play below it.

Playing below the point of decision, as victims do, means blaming other

2 Stephen Covey. The 7 Habits of Highly Effective People: Powerful Lessons in Personal Change,by Stephen Covey, first published in 1989 by Free Press. It has sold more than 25 million copiesworldwide. https://en.wikipedia.org/wiki/The_7_Habits_of_Highly_Effective_People

people, coming up with excuses, and denying the reality of what you've done or decided. Victims believe their lack of progress is due to their team, their poor business performance is the fault of the economy, and the current situation has nothing to do with them.

On the other hand, the victor plays above the point of decision. They take ownership of the situation, are accountable for their results, and responsible for their actions. They don't hide behind others, they act without excuses, and deal with how things are.

Good leaders are victors, living their lives above the point. They offer solutions instead of excuses. They say what they can do and do what they say, and don't talk about what they can't do. They hold themselves accountable for their actions, decisions, and results.

Unfortunately, the world has taught us to live below the point without meaning to do so. Just think of the news: most of the information that's broadcast is below-the-point news. That's the reason this way of thinking seems normal.

It isn't.

We suggest you stop watching the news and live above the point, as a victor. Take ownership of your success, your mindset, and your actions. Take responsibility for your life. It can be difficult recognizing when you're acting below the point, so don't get discouraged and don't give up.

Recognize common below-the-point behaviors and change them.

ABOVE-THE-POINT VICTOR BEHAVIORS Do this:	BELOW-THE-POINT VICTIM BEHAVIORS Instead of:
Talk to the person by phone (good) or in person (better).	Hiding behind an email
Ask questions to understand what's going on, focusing on facts	Making assumptions and jumping down people's throats
Find and offer or implement a solution that improves the situation	Quitting or complaining
Ask yourself how you could improve, grow, or learn	Making it someone else's problem
Choose to learn about and accommodate other people's styles to get the job done	Refusing to adapt or interact with others and expecting them to adjust for you

Leading by (bad) example

In recent years, a string of high profile scandals that tarnished the reputations of some large companies — Zenefits, Wells Fargo, ANZ Bank, Mitsubishi, Volkswagen, Toshiba, among others — rocked the business world.[3]

A common feature of these cases was that, in most cases, executives and upper management created or fostered toxic work cultures that encouraged unethical business practices such as cutting corners and worse to meet performance metrics that were set impossibly high.

It took strong leaders to create those conditions. Many leaders are passionate and charismatic, which influences others to follow them. But these environments developed and flourished because no one took ownership of them or responsibility for their actions or was accountable. Everyone went along to go along.

Strong leaders are not necessarily good leaders. Strength, passion, and charisma don't make a good leader.

Intentionality does.

Leading is passion and focus

Instead of the term leadership, let's use the verb leading because we're talking about actions. John C. Maxwell says

---

3 Steffen Maier, "The Top Five HR Trends for 2017," Steffen Maier, Fast Company, January 6,2017. https://www.fastcompany.com/3066976/the-top-five-hr-trends-for-2017.

that the key to effective leading is using a position's influence, not its authority.[4] Effective leaders encourage people to think for themselves, engage employees by teaching them how to follow-through on their initiative, and inspire confidence to try new things.

> ## *LEADERSHIP IS NOT ABOUT POSITION. IT'S ABOUT ACTION.*

Good leaders foresee the results of their decisions and understand the consequences. They take responsibility for their actions and those of their team. Their activities are intentional and deliberate: they do what they say they'll do. They possess self-control and self-discipline and respond to others thoughtfully and considerately.

Most importantly, good leaders develop other good leaders.

Imagine the value you'd add to your company if everyone who works for you were encouraged to develop the traits shared by good leaders, such as these:

---

4 John C. Maxwell, " Factors that Influence Influence," July 8, 2013 blog post, http://www.johnmaxwell.com/blog/7-factors-that-influence-influence

TRAITS OF *GOOD* LEADERS	TRAITS OF *POOR* LEADERS
Confidence, inner strength, and humility	Stubbornness, paranoia, and fear
Asking questions and listening to the answers	Talking too much
Clear and proactive communication	Expecting others to read minds
Always putting the team first	Blaming others for problems, throwing people under the bus
Creating a dialogue with others: When will you have...? What ideas do you have regarding...? What options do we have in solving this challenge?	Telling others what to do or offering no direction at all
Basing relationships on understanding other people	Making relationships transactional: I need you to do this for me.
There is an equal ratio of commitment and follow through	Making promises and not delivering on them
Seeing the big picture	Thinking about the here and now without considering tomorrow

TRAITS OF *GOOD* LEADERS	TRAITS OF *POOR* LEADERS
Including and involving others	Selfish in actions and thoughts
Self-driven	Expecting others to motivate them
Taking ownership of problems and challenges	Foisting work and blame onto others
Teaching people to think and look for solutions	Disparaging the ideas of others
Having an abundance mentality	Having a scarcity mentality
Balancing logic and emotion	Living on emotion: a diva

While there are positions in your company that require great leadership, it doesn't automatically come with the job. It must be developed and nurtured, which means that the company should define the leadership traits required for every position: after all, you want everyone to model them.

If the company wants every employee to have certain traits, it needs to put processes in place that will do that. It needs to develop and nurture talent.

> *CONTRARY TO THE*
> *OPINION OF MANY*
> *PEOPLE, LEADERS ARE*
> *NOT BORN. LEADERS ARE*
> *MADE, AND THEY ARE*
> *MADE BY EFFORT AND*
> *HARD WORK.*
> *— VINCE LOMBARDI [5]*

John C. Maxwell, in his *The 21 Irrefutable Laws of Leadership*[6], says that we need to lead ourselves before we lead others. Ask yourself: Would you follow you? His point, simply stated, is that Leadership = Influence. Or, to put it another way, be all you can be … and take some others with you. According to Maxwell, these seven factors identify the potential to emerge as a leader.

1. CHARACTER –
Who They Are

True leadership always begins with the inner person. The character of a leader begins with their heart and will filter into the entire organization and its employees. Great character creates potential for a great organization.

---

5 From a speech delivered by Vince Lombardi on June 22, 1970 in Dayton, Ohio.http://www.pnbhs.school.nz/wp-content/uploads/2015/11/VINCE-LOMBARDI-The-Speech-Leadership.pdf.
6 John C. Maxwell, "As a leader, the first person I need to lead is me" from The 21 Iirrefutable Laws of Leadership, p.age 162, by John C. Maxwell, (Thomas Nelson Books, 1998).

2. RELATIONSHIPS –
Who They Know

Build the right kinds of relationships
with the right people,
and you can become
the real leader in
an organization.
In your sphere
of influence,
you must develop
deep, meaningful
relationships that go beyond working in the same
office. Relationships grow loyalty, influence, and
ultimately, the business.

3. KNOWLEDGE –
What They Know

Whenever I was new to an
organization, I always spent a
lot of time doing homework
before I tried to take the
lead. New environments
bring about questions to
be answered. By seeking
knowledge before demanding a
leadership position, leaders have the chance
to learn first, lead second.

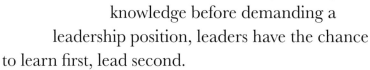
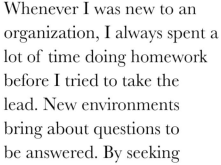

4. INTUITION –
What They Feel

Leaders seek to recognize and influence intangibles such as energy, morale, timing, and momentum. Leaders see past the obvious into realms that others cannot, and this affects the organization and its people as they can steer momentum down the best path with the most reward.

5. EXPERIENCE –
Where They've Been

The greater challenges you've faced as a leader in the past, the more likely followers are to give you a chance in the present. A leader's experience in navigating tough obstacles in the past can cause followers to appreciate where they can take the organization in the future.

6. PAST SUCCESS –
What They've Done

Every time I extended myself, took a risk, and succeeded, followers had another reason to trust my leadership

ability – and to listen to what I had to say. While success in the past doesn't guarantee the same in the future, it does make people feel more comfortable with being led and influenced. Find ways to take on challenges and excel in them, and you'll soon be presented with new responsibilities and leadership opportunities.

7. ABILITY –
What They Can Do

The bottom line for followers is what a leader is capable of. They want to know whether that person can lead the team to victory. When you show that you can lead a team to victory, you'll have shown you can positively influence your followers and organization.

TALENT DEVELOPMENT

Talent Development is a journey, not a destination.

Talent Development is helping everyone who works for the organization, from top management to frontline employees, continually develop and improve the hard and soft skills needed for short-term and long-term goals. It's a fundamental value for any company.

> *TRAIN PEOPLE WELL ENOUGH SO THEY CAN LEAVE; TREAT THEM WELL ENOUGH SO THEY DON'T WANT TO.*
> *— RICHARD BRANSON*[7]

Successful companies continually adapt to developing situations by continuously cultivating the skills and talents of their people to ensure that everyone who works in the organization can address new challenges as they arise or even before they appear.

The strategy is to guarantee that everyone's ready for their next position before they move into it, providing employees with stimulating, rewarding and challenging careers, and increasing their job engagement and satisfaction. This is important.

According to the Bellevue, Washington, mentoring firm Chronus, 79% of business and HR leaders worldwide believe they have a significant retention and engagement problem, with four out of 10 workers feeling disengaged.

7 From a post by Richard Branson on the Virgin website, March 27, 2014. www.virgin.com/richard-branson/look-after-your-staff

Furthermore, the primary reason people quit their jobs is a lack of future career opportunities. [8]

Well-trained team members can effortlessly move into new positions within the company as they're needed, so a business of any size can nimbly engage in new strategies to cope with paradigm shifts. The company can take risks by assembling new teams to tackle new problems, saving the time, money and effort of attracting new talent.

Yet, during the economic crisis in 2009, a survey revealed that two-thirds of responding employers felt the primary challenge facing them in the coming year was developing high-performing teams, and that there was a pressing need to identify and develop the potential of existing employees. [9]

A great workforce requires identifying the leadership traits the company needs in every position, defining the behaviors and skills you want people to learn and develop, and then modeling those behaviors yourself: great leaders lead by example, as previously described.

8 From the website for Chronus, a company that specializes in mentoring software. https://chronus.com/employee-development
9 Personnel Today, 5 May 2009.

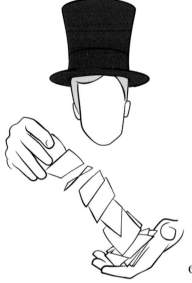

For employees to fully embrace personal growth as the company's culture, the process must begin at the highest level, demonstrating that anyone at any level and any stage can improve. An excellent first step in this direction is hiring an executive leadership business coach to help top-level employees develop the management and leadership skills they'll model for everyone else in the company.

Topics for development could include:

- Giving and receiving feedback

- Developing technical skills

- Learning people skills

- Developing leadership traits

- How to effectively manage processes

- Strategic thinking and execution planning

It's crucial for an organization's top-level people to continually support Talent Development programs and their outcomes. If these initiatives don't become part of the company's DNA, old habits win out over the initial enthusiasm of a new approach.

Energized employees become disengaged when they realize mandatory meetings that require them to check off boxes to prove attendance have replaced their potential for a better future.

Talent Development isn't an after-thought, tacked onto the schedules if time allows. It is part of a company's foundation and core strategy, incorporated into its structure, and as such should have time and space allocated to it for workshops or training sessions in proportion to their importance.

Talent Development involves creating a documented plan based on the following six points to which the organization commits:

- a specific and strategic approach to Talent Development;

- a culture of continuous improvement;

- a culture that promotes leadership and abundance thinking;

- the creation of a Talent Development plan that identifies future leaders and structures their training;

- helping every employee write their personal training plan designed to prepare them for advancement or growth within the company;

- reviewing employee progress after each training session.

Other Approaches to Developing Talent

Talent development is a continual, pervasive process. It can and should be developed outside the formal setting of conference rooms and classrooms because people learn just as much in informal surroundings.

People have different learning styles, and on-the-job training gives employees chances to see theory in practice. Lunch and learns and internal and external workshops are chances for team members to learn while developing interpersonal relationships with people from other departments or companies. If people need a pressure-free learning environment, consider home-study courses.

Other innovative approaches to develop talent are:

Change performance reviews to personal development plans. A simple name change promotes the positive aspects of coaching and growing. The emphasis is on future possibilities rather than past mistakes.

Establish a company library. Publish a continually updated list of suggested books that could have impact on employees' learning. Start a book club so everyone can read the same book and discuss how to apply its concepts.

Analyzing Performance

A manager is responsible for maximizing results by challenging workers to deliver consistent quality performances. A manager who settles for less-than-acceptable performance from any member of the team, for whatever reason, is not doing right by either the company or the team. A manager who allows poor performance to continue without confronting those responsible creates an environment that breeds anchors who drag down the rest of the team. As a result, the manager contributes to the failure of everyone on the team instead of caring enough to motivate them to do and be their best. Allowing poor performance is damning the team's future and not just with the company: it signals individuals that they are not worth the time or effort to help, or that they're incapable of doing better.

When adjustments are needed, it's crucial to give feedback in appropriate and useful ways.

Giving Feedback

Giving feedback can be difficult. It can be painful, embarrassing, or uncomfortable to talk to people about things that are wrong, that need to improve, that need to change. In many cases, this fear on the part of a manager can lead to no feedback at all, with dire results for the goals of the company and the advancement of the team member concerned. Part of the problem is that feedback deals with past performance though its purpose is to change future behaviors. Feedback is a coaching opportunity, not a blame-game.

Here are three approaches to giving feedback that range from adjusting the usual approach to the BEER behavior modification system, to Marshall Goldsmith's fun and helpful Feed*Forward* solution.

OPTION 1: ADJUST YOUR STANDARD FEEDBACK METHOD

NO FEEDBACK
The worst feedback of all.

It can mean no news is good news, or I guess they don't care, or boy, I must be in trouble, they won't even talk to me.

STRAIGHT FEEDBACK

Tells it like it is, just the facts. This can be taken as positive or negative, but it's generally not neutral. *Example: You have a goal of $1,000,000 in business by year end. It's September, and you're at 50%.*

NEGATIVE FEEDBACK

4 times more effective than no feedback. *Example: I'm not pleased with how you follow up with customers. People are starting to leave because of poor service. Tell me how you plan to improve.*

POSITIVE REINFORCING FEEDBACK

<u>10 times more effective than no feedback.</u> *Example: I'm very impressed with how you relate to your customers and your prompt service. This will keep customers coming in. Keep it up! Great job!*

OPTION 2: ADJUST A TEAM MEMBER'S BEHAVIOR

The BEER concept focuses on giving thoughtful advice to modify behavior while avoiding personal remarks. When preparing to advise a team, check that each point you want to make addresses the following:

- **Behavior** – What the individual is doing or not doing that is unacceptable.

- **Effect** – Why the behavior is unacceptable, how it hurts productivity, bothers others, limits sales, etc.

- **Expectation** – What you expect the individual to do or not do.

- **Result** – What will happen if the individual changes (positive tone) or the consequences of this behavior continuing (negative tone).

OPTION 3: MARSHALL GOLDSMITH'S FEEDFORWARD

Feed*Forward* can be a one-on-one conversation or a group exercise. Its purpose is to provide individuals with suggestions for the future and help them achieve a positive change in the behaviors they select. Aside from its effectiveness and efficiency, Feed*Forward* can make life a lot more enjoyable so there are many times when it's preferable to feedback in day-to-day interactions.

In the Feed*Forward* process, people are asked to:

- Choose to change one behavior to make a positive difference in their lives.

- Describe this behavior to others.

- Ask for two suggestions for achieving a positive change in the behavior.

- Listen to suggestions and take notes without commenting on them.

- Thank others for their suggestions.

- Ask others what they would like to change.

- Provide Feed*Forward* — two suggestions aimed at helping them change.

- Say, "you are welcome" when thanked for the suggestions.

Giving and receiving feedforward only takes about two minutes. When asked to describe this experience, people use words like great, energizing, useful, helpful, fun.

Quality communication between and among people at all levels and every department and division is the glue that holds organizations together. By using feedforward and encouraging others to use it, leaders can dramatically improve the quality of communication in their organizations while ensuring they have conveyed the right message and those who receive it are receptive to its content. The result is a much more dynamic and open organization -- one whose employees focus on the promise of the future rather than dwelling on the mistakes of the past.

RECRUITMENT

It's not always possible to find the talent you need in-house, so you need to track down the people who not only make your success possible but inevitable. Then you must convince them to work for you.

A clear hiring and recruitment process is well-documented, with well-defined steps to follow each time a new team member needs to be hired. It's designed to bring in the people who are a perfect fit for the company in general and the job in particular.

The perfect fit is not so much about technical skills — they can always be taught and polished — than cultural fit, how well a candidate matches the company's core values and can help meet the demands of today's challenging business environment. This is getting harder, as perfect talent is becoming more elusive and demanding, leading some companies to make do with less-than-perfect hires.

This is not new, according to Isaac Getz, professor at ESCP Europe Business School and co-author of Freedom Inc. Attracting top talent is a continual challenge for HR directors, he says, but what is new are the ways some companies are starting to tackle these challenges. The old ways such as signing bonuses and incentives work less and less in a VUCA world.[10] VUCA stands for Volatility, Uncertainty, Complexity, and Ambiguity

> **Volatility:** challenges are not necessarily hard to understand or learn about, but they are unexpected, unstable, and may be of unknown duration; solutions are often expensive. For example, prices fluctuate when a natural disaster takes a supplier offline.

---

10 The notion of VUCA was introduced by the U.S. Army War College to describe the more volatile, uncertain, complex and ambiguous multilateral world that came about at the end of the Cold War. The term VUCA became more common in the 1990s and has been used widely in the field of strategic leadership. https://en.wikipedia.org/wiki/Volatility,_uncertainty,_complexity_and_ambiguity .com/richard-branson/look-after-your-staff.

Uncertainty: while an event's underlying cause
   and effect are known, other information is lacking,
   making change possible but not inevitable. For
   instance, a competitor's pending product launch
   muddies the future of the business and the market.

Complexity: the situation has many
   interconnected parts and variables; information
   is available or predictable but processing it can be
   overwhelming. For example, you're doing business
   in many countries, each with unique regulatory
   environments, tariffs, and cultural values.

Ambiguity: Causal relationships are entirely
   unclear; no precedents exist so there are unknown
   unknowns. For instance, you decide to move
   into immature or emerging markets or to launch
   products outside your core competencies.

VUCA environments
are rapidly enveloping
even stable nations because
of sharp and rapid
technological changes, people's
unease with social changes,
significant political disagreements
within and between countries,
terrorism and war in a highly
interconnected world, the
pressure on natural resources,
and global warming.

In a VUCA world, carefully laid plans often don't survive contact with hard reality. This is a problem for recruiting techniques that favor those who plan well and execute plans brilliantly. In the face of emerging business realities, good business strategies need to supplant original plans and goals with new ones, and recruiters need to assess an applicant's ability to sense and respond to these new realities, or to learn from them.

Planning and execution are still relevant when facing VUCA, but they're baseline requirements. More critical are three other capabilities:

- The ability to sense, on the fly, the reality of a situation.

- The ability to respond effectively to the sensed reality, even without resources to assess significant implications carefully.

- The ability to learn rapidly from experience and incorporate the lessons into plans, execution, and most importantly, the building of sense and respond capabilities.[11]

The perfectly-fitting candidate doesn't just have to match the current company culture: they'll need to match a culture that changes as the company evolves. People who can adapt on the fly like this can find a home anywhere, a challenge for recruiters who must sell your business to them.

_____

11 Personnel Today, 5 May 2009 /hr-topics/talent-acquisition/pages/how-to-recruit-prepare-leaders-vuca-world.aspx. Society for Human Resource Management. Accessed 1/20/18.

This is no time for false modesty. Applicants, even unicorns, are hungry to hear what life could be like working with you, so take the time to make the details as exciting as possible. Create an emotional connection, clearly describing the role(s) you're offering and their responsibilities and expected outcomes, the company's plans, and how the candidate will support and be supported by the company's mission.

Paul Petrone, writing on the LinkedIn Talent Blog, suggests the following reasons top talent find it hard to commit to you and offers methods for inducing them to join you:

> **The best candidates are deciding between multiple offers at once.** So, make the interview as excellent an experience as possible, involve the prospective manager in the meeting, and introduce a senior leader to the applicant.
>
> **There's too much noise in the market.** Counter this with a reliable employer brand, strong purpose during the interview, and a described path for advancement.
>
> **There's a shortage of great talent.** Research the best places to recruit and adopt a data-driven approach to the process.
>
> **Hiring managers are too picky about what they want.** Develop a healthy relationship with your hiring manager.[12]

---

12 Paul Petrone, "4 of the Biggest Problems Recruiters Face (And How to Overcome Them)," byPaul Petrone, December 3, 2015; https://business.linkedin.com/talent-solutions/blog/recruiting-ips/2015/4-of-the-biggest-problems-recruiters-face-and-how-to-overcome-them.

THE ADDING ZEROS 10-STEP RECRUITING PROCESS

The recruiting process is mostly a test, with the company offering the job to the top-scorer in all areas. Candidates respond to an ad by a given date, complete a DISC profile, and answer questions that reveal whether they fit the position and the company's culture.

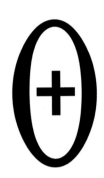

STEP 1.
Review or update the position.

Every position in every organization should know whether they're successful. Make sure that the position clearly describes the responsibilities of the role, as well as the measurable expectations of success and the behavioral characteristics the role requires. If I don't know what success in my position looks like, how do I know if I'm successful in my responsibilities.

STEP 2.
Advertise the position.

A job advertisement sells the company just as much if not more than an ad designed for its products. The announcement positions the job as the solution to a need the candidate didn't necessarily know they had. In addition to selling the company, the ad needs to specify minimum skill requirements and an application process with a deadline date.

STEP 3.
Review Résumés.

After the deadline passes, filter out the applicants who don't meet the minimum experience requirement and don't offer a good fit with the company culture.

STEP 4.
Screen hopefuls by phone.

Confirm their experience and ask a few questions that reveal their fit with the company culture. Use the answers to narrow your list to the top two to four names.

STEP 5. Invite the top candidates to interview.

Ask interviewees to complete a DISC[13] behavioral profile in advance. A DISC behavioral profile enables you to evaluate their behaviors in their areas of strength as well as any areas that might be of concern. They should return them early enough that you have time to use them in the interview.

13 Find one here: www.123test.com/disc-behavior-test/

STEP 6.

Start the interivew with the company's story.

Break the ice with the company's history, purpose, core values, and the future direction of the company. Then describe the position for which the candidate is interviewing, with the objective of wowing them with who you are and where you're headed. Remember: you must do just as much selling as the applicant does.

STEP 7.

Question Time.

Ask questions that relate to the company's core values and the behavioral characteristics needed for this position to be successful. You're looking for the traits that you've identified are needed for success in this position. Focus on past behaviors. Ask about events on their resume. Tell me about the time when you … Don't ask what if questions: predicting the future isn't helpful in this case.

STEP 8. Rate The Candidate.

It's important that two company people are present at each interview. Both interviewers take notes and rate each candidate response on a scale of 1 to 5. After you've completed all the interviews, this will be used to review and rank the candidates.

STEP 9. Contact References.

Many companies will not provide references for employees for several reasons, yet this information is critical in the hiring process. Circumvent these policies by asking the candidate to set up a phone appointment with someone they have worked with in the past. If the position involved leadership responsibilities have the candidate set up an appointment with someone they have led.

STEP 10. Make the Offer.

Make the offer to the candidate that best fits the role, behavioral, characteristics and core values.

If the company has carefully identified the team member traits it believes are necessary (see **Leadership**), it should now be relatively simple to identify the best candidate for the position: not using gut feelings, but data like the interviewer's graded responses and the DISC behavior profile. As you develop a job's description and its requirements, it's a good idea to build in the DISC behavioral profile that would be best suited to it.

The DISC behavioral profile is a system of behavior analysis that can be used to predict a person's behavior when they work alone or with others.[14] It's useful for identifying a person's dominant behavior type among four possible categories: Dominant, Influential, Steady, Compliant.

D (Dominant) behavior types enjoy competition and challenge. They're goal-oriented and want others to recognize them for their efforts and achievements. They aim high, want authority and are resourceful and adaptable. They are usually self-sufficient and individualistic, losing interest in projects once the challenge is gone. Dominant behavior types tend to be impatient with minor details. They are usually direct and self-confident, enjoy being the center of attraction, and may take it for granted that people think highly of them. They may tend to be somewhat critical of others.

---

14 DISC is a behavior assessment tool based on work by American psychologist William MoultonMarston. It centers on four different behavioral traits: dominance, inducement, submission, and compliance. It was further developed into a behavioral assessment tool by industrial psychologist Walter Vernon Clarke.

Consequently, other people may tend to see them as being slightly domineering and overpowering.

Dominant behavior types like to be leaders. Respect them and never make them feel inferior.

I (Influential) behavior types are very interested in meeting and being with people. They are optimistic, outgoing, and socially skilled, and are quick at establishing relationships. Sometimes their concern for people and their feelings may make them reluctant to disturb a favorable situation or relationship.

Influential behavior types want to be friends, not a boss or employee. Relate to them by talking to them about things in their lives; build relationships.

S (Steady) behavior types are usually patient, calm and controlled. They are very willing to help others, particularly those they consider friends. They can deal with the task at hand and perform routine work with patience and care. They're happier sticking to methods that have proved successful in the past.

Steady behavior types are well-liked because they are friendly, easy-going and harmless. However, they're harder to work with than Dominant or Influential sorts because they don't like pressure or pushy people. Be casual and reserved with them, outline what you want them to do, but don't expect quick decisions.

C (**Compliant**) **behavior types** are detail and process-oriented. They are cautious rather than impulsive and avoid taking risks. They are tactful and diplomatic and strive for a stable, ordered life. Compliant behavior types have a high acceptance of rules and regulations and feel comfortable following procedures in both business and their personal lives.

Compliant behavior types can be challenging to manage. They're skeptical of authority and wary of change, so they'll procrastinate and ask a lot of questions. Give them details and time to make decisions.

If you've looked for yourself in this list, you've realized that all of us are a combination of all four types in various proportions, so bear this in mind during recruitment. Additionally, people often change their natures when under tense circumstances.

Under pressure, a Dominant behavior can become a Compliant behavior, meaning they'll be more considerate of details and think carefully before making a decision. A Dominant behavior could also turn into a Steady behavior, slowing down and grounding themselves. In other words, a behavior trait that may seem undesirable could be precisely the one you want in the clutch.

An Influential behavior can become a Dominant behavior under stress, bossing everyone around without much regard for their feelings instead of being friendly. This can be very disconcerting, like Dr. Jekyll and Mr. Hyde, and troublesome in the workplace. An Influential behavior could also become a Steady behavior, growing more reserved, slowing down and thinking more deliberately.

A Steady behavior could become a Dominant one under the gun, which means they'll act and think quickly, maybe even loudly barking out orders, the mouse that roars.

A Compliant behavior could become a Dominant one, thinking and acting more quickly than usual.

When taking all these possibilities into account, consider who's already in position and would work with the new hire: could a department full of Dominant types be able to function? Could a team composed of Influential behaviors ever get anything done?

DISC is a powerful business tool for developing effective communication skills. If you're communicating with an employee, but you're not clear in your actions and they don't perform the way you want them to, you weren't clear in your communication. A good communicator knows it's their responsibility to be clear, not the responsibility of the other to decipher and understand.

TRUE COMMUNICATION IS THE RESPONSE YOU GET. YOU KNOW YOU'RE COMMUNICATING EFFECTIVELY WHEN YOU GET THE RESPONSE YOU DESIRE.

The best communicators adapt to whom they're talking to, and DISC helps you become a great adapter, learning to adjust to other people's styles to get the responses you need. The objective is to be a high DISC, meaning that you adapt to those with whom you're communicating. The ideal scenario is when both communicators adapt to each other's style, meeting in the middle to get what they need.

Onboarding: it ain't over yet

A new employee gains a more rounded understanding of the organization when they learn about their new role and the company's values, strategy and purpose. This makes their first few weeks at the company a relationship-building opportunity while they're getting training and the tools they need for success. This is the purpose of onboarding.

Onboarding is a documented process created by Human Resources and the new hire's manager. The onboarding plan describes what is to be taught to the new employee and by whom. It contains a timeline for when this is to happen and provides metrics and benchmarks for proficiency, as well as a schedule for when the new hire is to meet those standards.

If they don't meet the benchmarks, dig deep to find out why. Was the training clear and effective? Is the person willing or able to follow the instruction? Is there a bad fit of either culture or experience?

Onboarding is not a single event like an orientation meeting; it's a process that extends throughout the induction process.

It's part of the company's culture of Talent Development that continues throughout an employee's tenure with the organization.

As such, the essential onboarding trends, as noted by Top Employers Institute, look a lot like best practices for Talent Development:

Process, not event. Instead of a standard two- or three-day experience, onboarding should continue for three to six months after the job starts.

Moving towards a multi-dimensional program. Onboarding should cover the business context (our purpose, goals, and other information that gives them a powerful understanding of who we are and where we're going) the situational context (the job and its expectations), and the cultural context (core values).

Senior management is actively involved. This helps in the understanding of the overall business purpose and direction.

Gain insight. Data collection enables the measurement of employees' progress, and program improvements, impact, and effectiveness.[15]

15 Caitlin Drysdale, "The Top 5 Current Onboarding Trends," by Caitlin Drysdale, HR Grapevine, May 23, 2016, citing Eleanor Nickerson, Director of UK Operations for Top Employers Institute; https://www.hrgrapevine.com/content/article/2016-05-23-the-top-five-current-on-boarding-trends.

You build trust with new hires during their first few weeks, which is your opportunity to prove to them that they made the right decision in joining you. You also gain valuable insight into them and what they have to offer the company — and sometimes you discover that they don't offer that much. You realize you've both made a mistake.

If so, it's time to look for a new team member. Remember this Talent Development standard: hire slow, fire fast.

THE MAGIC OF ADDING ZEROS THROUGH PEOPLE

It can be tempting to think of a magical workforce that needs little to no supervision, never complains, and is completely interchangeable: robots, in other words.

But robots will never replace the human mind's curiosity and problem-solving abilities, not to mention our empathy for other humans. If the Sorcerer's Apprentice had been a good leader, he wouldn't have started up a process he didn't know how to stop. Furthermore, the broom would have known that success looked like a cauldron full of water and known when to stop.

As you've seen in this chapter, leadership is not a skill that automatically shows up with a job title; it's a set of behaviors that must be taught and learned. It's important work because of the way in which it touches people's lives and makes them feel about themselves as well as the company. It's a responsibility that's not to be taken lightly.

When an organization leads its team with intentionality, it has real benefits for its constituents.

PEOPLE	
Team Members *high morale staff retention*	Customers *well trained staff adding value*

Team Members benefit from high morale and staff retention, and Customers benefit from always working with people who value them and their loyalty.

As you saw in this chapter, the Discipline of People increases stability through:

- **leadership** that creates passionate and focused people who think for themselves, follow-through on their initiative, and are confident in trying new things;

- **talent development** that cultivates skills and behaviors to ensure that we are maximizing our strengths and reaching our goals;

- **recruitment** that makes success inevitable.

Business is ultimately about bringing two groups of people together: those who have needs and those who can meet those needs. To solve a problem well for another person requires human interaction, empathy, and initiative.

The organization that consistently ensures its team members have everything they need to excel in these areas will always outperform mindless robots who will never be able to say "us" instead of "you" when referring to their company.

CHAPTER **10**
CONSISTENCY: THE INCANTATION

ADDING ZEROS THROUGH THE DISCIPLINE OF EXECUTION

ABRACADABRA!
OPEN SESAME!
SHAZAM!

The performance of magic almost always involves the use of language, whether spoken aloud or unspoken, to access or guide magical power.

An incantation or spell is a specific set of words in a specific order. Say them out of order and nothing happens. Forget to wave your wand at the right time or in the right direction and instead of a dove flying out of a hat, a pigeon poops in your eye. But when the words and accompanying actions are right, the audience is wowed.

It's like a recipe: certain ingredients in specified proportions, mixed and handled in a particular order will result in a chocolate cake. Change any of that information and you might end up with a cake … or a mess. Good cooks and good magicians know that performing the same actions in the same order always obtains the same result. They've labored over every detailed step to perfect the outcome and then learned those steps by heart until they are habit. And if for some reason they're unable to perform those steps, they can hand the entire documented process to someone else who can then deliver consistent results.

HABITS>PROCESSES>CONSISTENCY

When we find consistency in an organization, we'll discover that the company has habits that guide their processes, financials, and management. Habits are the basis of processes that give freedom to workers because the focus shifts from the individual to the entire business, protecting the company's financial controls. Good organizational habits can eliminate poor communication, one of the most significant challenges in the corporate world.

When a company habitually meets with team members in daily huddles, report - outs, and feedback sessions, that means it's helping employees contribute to the long - term well - being of the organization without even thinking about it - good communication is automatic and expected. Habits like these ensure that a team can execute its strategy with absolute consistency.

How to add zeros to Execution

You can increase consistency by implementing these three components of the Discipline of Execution:

- Processes

- Management

- Financial Controls

Let's look at each of these now in detail to see how they enable efficiency and effectiveness.

PROCESSES

Without documented processes in place, a business relies entirely on the skills of the workers who produce the best work. If workers have varying degrees of ability, the company delivers a varying quality of product. This does not lead to longevity. The loss of the most skilled workers will lead to the loss of whatever customers the company has managed to satisfy.

Instead of relying on workers alone, businesses need to rely on skilled workers who maximize outcomes by following proven processes.

A process is a sequence of interdependent, linked procedures which, at every stage, consume one or more resources (employee time, energy, machines, money) to convert inputs (data, material, parts, etc.) into outputs. These outputs then serve as inputs for the next stage until a known goal or result is reached.[1]

---

1 http://www.businessdictionary.com/definition/process.html.

SOLVE EVERY PROBLEM WITH A PROCESS.

Many companies believe they have processes in place because they work through a series of steps through force of mental habit - this happens, then this happens, then we get those results. But this is a schedule, not a process. A process has clear documented steps and it has clear expectations of what the results of each step should be so everyone knows when it's time to move on to the next step, and what the entire process looks like when it's complete. It's not enough to say, yeah, that looks good.

According to surgeon Atul Gawande, failure in the modern world results from errors of ineptitude (mistakes we make because we don't make proper use of what we know) rather than errors of ignorance (mistakes we make because we don't know enough).

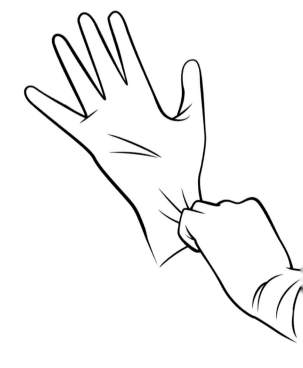

In his powerful and thought - provoking book, *The Checklist Manifesto*, he shows how the routine tasks of surgeons have now become so incredibly complicated that it's just too easy for an otherwise competent doctor to miss a step, or forget to ask a key question or, in the stress and pressure of the moment, to fail to plan properly for every eventuality, making mistakes all but inevitable. After researching other professions where errors have grave consequences, he came up with a solution, experts need checklists – literally – written guides that walk them through the key steps in any complex procedure. His safe surgery checklist is now in place around the world and has achieved staggering successv.[2]

If highly trained surgeons — surgeons! — need checklists to make certain they've remembered to wash their hands, think about what happens when the company brings someone new into their process. For as long as it takes for the new hire to develop correct habits, their work product will be different from everyone else's. How does the company ensure that those newly learned habits are the correct ones and the same as everyone else's?

2 Atul Gawande, "The Checklist Manifesto: How to Get Things Right," by Atul Gawande; http://atulgawande.com/book/the-checklist-manifesto/.

Realistically speaking, if the company hasn't documented its process, everyone's work product is different. No matter how routine, without definitive checkpoints to ensure conformity, different people will do different things on different days if it's not written down.

IF THE PROCESS ISN'T WRITTEN DOWN, IT DOESN'T EXIST.

In any given business there are likely between six and twelve primary processes. Typical financial processes take care of payroll, accounts receivable and accounts payable. There should be processes for sales, marketing, fulfillment, talent management, and manufacturing. Each step of each process requires a responsible person who ensures the procedure is followed, is on schedule, and is completed to the correct standard.

In your company, do these vital processes have a documented flow-chart or checklist that ensures consistency and responsibility, or do they depend on the habits of the employees who carry them out?

Your company may have its ways of doing things that developed on the spur of the moment in the early days when routines grew out of necessity. That may have worked then, but it's time to look for better ways.

Sometimes this works, but why leave things to chance?

How to document a process in 4 steps

To create a process in any department or part of the company, document how workers do things now. It's first crucial to get a thorough understanding of how things are being done now, from corporate routines to individual habits, departmental timelines to implementation procedures.

First: write down what you do right now. If multiple people do the same thing, pay attention to the person who does it the most. To document the current steps, you can:

- have someone write steps down as they watch the person doing them;

- have the person performing the steps write them as they do them;

- have a trainee write them down as their trainer does them.

Second: evaluate the steps to make sure they cover everything that needs to be accomplished. Edit as needed, adding, adjusting, or subtracting as needed.

Third: challenge the newly developed steps and expected outcomes. Bring together the team members who are responsible for performing the process you are working on. Discuss your testing and the steps that need to change in your process, and the outcomes that they need to achieve. Have them use the process exactly as written. Then test the new process with a few people for 2 - 4 weeks, noting any adjustments that may be necessary at the end of that period.

Fourth: implement your notes, one item at a time, after the test period. Observe the impact, if any, that this has on the process and its outcomes. Once you've made the necessary adjustments, train the rest of the responsible team in the new process.

As the new process now has a set list of steps and expectations, consistency depends on workers following that list to the letter. Checking off each step as it's completed means there is accountability - did the process fail for some unknown reason, or because someone didn't do what they were supposed to do? In a process where different people perform each step, a checklist enables you to determine where the problem occurred.

Types of checklists include the following:

- **Task lists** are step-by-step inventories of standard operating procedures that people must follow in a specified order to achieve a pre-determined result.

- **Troubleshooting** lists outline the steps to take when things go wrong.

- **Coordination lists** are used to manage complex projects involving many people performing different tasks.

- **Discipline lists** catalogue procedures that prevent faulty decision-making.

- **To-do lists** are used to manage time and priorities.

Checklists are helpful in ensuring that people do things correctly and identifying who was responsible for things going off the rails. For this reason, lists and the processes they document may cause people to reject the process for a variety of reasons. But before you jump to conclusions and blame the individual involved, ask yourself four questions:

- *Did we train them on our process?*

- *Is our process correct?*

- *Is the employee willing to follow our process?*

- *What exactly is the process?*

The employee can only control one part of this - their willingness to follow the process. The other three are the responsibility of the organization and its managers.

An employee can't be held responsible for following a process that doesn't exist. And we find that when managers have no processes to manage, they try to manage people instead, leading them to complain that their team is unpredictable and wants to do things their way.

Of course, they do. Without a process, what other way is there?

Around 80% of what most employees do every day is the same, day in and day out. It becomes routine, which is good because routines free us from wasting mental energy on workaday tasks. When we're on autopilot, we can quickly do the things that crop up on a regular basis. This saves our brains for the other 20% of tasks that need some creativity to perform.

A good routine frees you from the endless series of small decisions that consume

time and energy and brings order and predictability to the day. And the things that don't happen regularly can still be made routine through processes that we consult when needed. That way, brain power is reserved for meaningful challenges.

MANAGEMENT

We can't say it often enough: management and leadership are two different things. Leadership creates passionate and focused people, management oversees processes, so the team is competent and productive.

WE DON'T MANAGE PEOPLE; WE MANAGE PROCESSES.

When processes are in place, there's something to manage. And while we don't manage people, we can and should manage their accountability.

Every organization needs good management and good leadership (See *Leadership* in Chapter 9). Managers, then, need to be the best suited for the job and an excellent fit for the organization, fitting in culturally and professionally.

They need to understand and be excited by the organization's purpose, direction, and culture.

Proper management balances processes and people, efficiency and humanity, without jeopardizing either one. When making a process decision, we should ask, how does this affect our people? And when making a people decision, we should ask, how does this affect our process? This is good management practice.

Good management practices aren't intuitive. Organizations need to use proven methods to teach managers fundamental and useful managerial techniques that include:

- selecting the right people for the team;

- delegating;

- flexibility;

- excellent verbal and non-verbal communication skills;

- managing communication processes such as daily huddles, one-to-one's, weekly team meetings, training, and feedback;

- recognizing the abilities of team members and allowing them to take ownership of and responsibility for their respective jobs.

As you can see from this list, good management is about being proactively helpful to the people they oversee. Nearly 75% of employees report they don't feel engaged in their jobs, while the remaining quarter says they have a good relationship with an immediate supervisor who's proactive in getting them involved and invested in their work.[3]

Proactive managers:

- provide feedback to team members;

- make time for team members;

- identify goals;

- act as role models;

- delegate;

- communicate;

- listen;

- motivate;

- set clear expectations;

- learn and adjust;

- recognize team members.

3 Dale Carnegie Institute, " Enhancing Employee Engagement: The Role of the Immediate Supervisor," Dale Carnegie Institute"; https://www.dalecarnegie.com/en/resources/enhancing- employee-engagement-the-role-of-the-immediate-supervisor

Forbes Magazine says great managers do five things every day:

1. They're straightforward.

2. They exhibit mature leadership.

3. They put the right people in the right positions.

4. They hold regular and meaningful one-to-one meetings.

5. They actively manage conflict.[4]

Meetings

Meetings have a bad reputation. Data reveals that 76% of participants are annoyed by meetings they consider a waste of time. Interestingly, though, there is a split along age-lines, with those under 34 likely to consider face-to-face meetings useful and productive, while those 35 and above mostly find them unnecessary. [5]

4 Kristi Hedges, "Five Things Great Managers Do Every Day," May 1, 2014, Forbes. https://www.forbes.com/sites/work-in-progress/2014/05/01/five-things-great-managers-do-every-day/#209db26e4109 .
5 Andrea Lehr, "Why We Hate Meetings So Much," HubSpot; https://blog.hubspot.com/sales/why-we-hate-meetings-so-much.

Regardless of individual preference, though, excellent managers review goals and actions by incorporating a process, a habit, and a rhythm for doing so. This takes the form of regular meetings to dig deep into issues, solve challenges, make decisions, update the status of action plans, and set priorities for specific periods of time.

There are three kinds of meetings that Management should hold on a regular basis with their team or department: weekly, monthly, and quarterly.

WEEKLY MEETINGS

The thing to remember is that the goals don't change, the actions do, so weekly meetings are to review and assess whether everything is on track to meet quarterly goals or whether actions need to change.

WEEKLY TEAM MEETINGS

Effective managers hold weekly 60-120-minute team meetings.

A useful technique to facilitate this is to color-code updates to make them easy to read as follows:

- **Green**: I'm on track with timelines and expected results

- **Yellow:** I am a little behind or my expected results are a bit behind but here is my plan to correct this

- **Red:** There is no way I will hit my deadlines or expected benchmarks; we need to adjust timing, reprioritize, or obtain additional resources to make it happen.

WEEKLY INDIVIDUAL MEETINGS

Effective managers have weekly or bi-weekly face-to-face or one-to-one phone meetings with individual team members to talk about progress on their 90-day action plan.

Effective managers facilitate the process of team members creating their individual 90-day action plans that outline their actions and important time-frames. The plans are built in reverse, starting with the goal to be achieved in 90 days and detailing who is responsible for specific outcomes and the metrics or measures that will be used to evaluate progress. This provides clarity regarding when specific actions will be complete.

The benefits of 90-day action plans include the following:

• it provides clarity about the steps needed to achieve the specified results;

• team members have clear objectives and clear processes to attain them;

• team members know when they need to start a task and when they need to complete it;

• it encourages the team member to anticipate and prepare;

• it enables planning to accommodate changes in schedules, such as vacations, conferences, trade shows, etc.

MONTHLY TEAM MEETINGS

Another powerful process is a monthly 2-3-hour review session to assess progress: [6]Are we on track for the current 90-day period? This session reviews financials, continually making appropriate adjustments to ensure they achieve the quarterly priorities and committed actions or 90-day action plans.

QUARTERLY MEETINGS

A quarterly meeting is a day-long session that typically has these objectives:

- review the previous quarter's results and action plans concerning the one-year and three-year goals;

- review the status of the Five Disciplines and how constituents are currently being satisfied;

- discuss the current priorities (company, department, individual);

- review the most critical numbers with relevant KPIs;

- identify the new goals and priorities for the upcoming quarter, including who's doing what by when so everyone can develop their new 90-day action plans.Following the quarterly meeting, managers share priorities with their teams and facilitate the creation of their team members' plans that support achieving goals and priorities.

---

6 See A Sample Agenda for Annual and Quarterly SessionA page 56,for detailed information about one- and three-year plans.

The funnel for execution starts with the 10-year, 3-year, and 1-year goals that senior management set during their annual Strategic Thinking and Execution Planning meeting, and leads to weekly meetings that review the progress toward those goals, as shown on the next page:

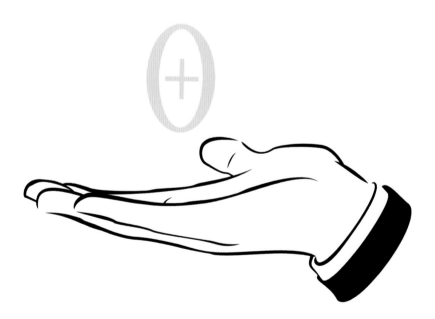

BIG HAIRY AUDACIOUS GOAL (BHAG)[7]

(10 years or more)

3-YEAR GOALS TOWARD ACHIEVING BHAG

Determine Goals for the 3-Year Benchmark

Identify 3-5 priorities to achieve the goals

1-YEAR GOALS
TOWARD ACHIEVING 3-YEAR GOAL

Determine Goals for the 1-Year Benchmark

Identify 3-5 priorities to achieve the goals

HOLD QUARTERLY MEETINGS

Determine Goals for the Upcoming Quarter

Identify 3-5 priorities to Achieve Those Goals

Create 90-Day Action Plans

CREATE INDIVIDUAL
90-DAY PLANS
FOR ACHIEVING 1-YEAR GOALS

Actions to accomplish those priorities

Target metrics for success

HOLD WEEKLY
TEAM /INDIVIDUAL
MEETINGS

Assess progress toward

Quarterly Goals/Action Plans

At the end of each period (weeks and quarters), rinse and repeat, just as you do for the annual meetings.

FINANCIAL CONTROLS

A company's financials are its story, its numbers. They include Income Statements, Balance Sheets, Statements of Cash Flow and Financial Ratios, on a monthly, quarterly and an annual basis. Comprehend those figures, and you'll know where the company has come from and where it's headed.

The sad reality is that many businesses just don't know their financials, even though every business executive, leader, and manager should be looking at them at least every week, if not daily.

To get an accurate picture of a company's progress toward its financial goals or to make required adjustments, we need real-time information (or as current as we can get).

According to research conducted by Aberdeen Group in 2014:[8]

- 35% of respondents indicated that demand for expedited financial information delivery is their top pressure.

7 "Big Hairy Audacious Goal" is a term proposed by James Collins and Jerry Porras in Built to Last: Successful Habits of Visionary Companies, 1994,(HarperBusiness, 1994). It encourages companies to define visionary goals that are more strategic and emotionally compelling.
8 Real-Time Financial Reporting: The Need for Speed, Aberdeen Group July 2014.

- Best-in-Class organizations are 62% more likely than all others to have real-time updates to financial metrics.

- The Best-in-Class are 2.7 times as likely as all others to have automated financial reporting including narrative analysis.

- Organizations with real-time access to financial performance can deliver information in time for decision-making 86% of the time.

Let's take a closer look at what these financial reports are:

Income Statement. Often referred to as a Statement of Profit and Loss, or P&L, this shows a company's generated revenues and incurred expenses over a specified period. It also shows the net gain or loss for the company during the stated accounting period.

Balance Sheet. This presents a snapshot of the company as of a single date, most often the last day of a quarter or year. It also shows the accounting value of all the company's assets, liabilities, and shareholder's equity as of that date.

Cash Flow Statement. This presents an analysis of all activities during the accounting period that affected cash, impacted primarily by operations, financing, and investments.

Financial Ratios. You calculate these from the reported figures in the financial statements. They're used to analyze the relative financial health of the company to gauge its improvement on its ratios. You can compare them over time within the same organization to spot trends and evaluate risks, especially when deviating from businesses in the same or similar risk categories.[9]

Six critical financial ratios for any business

Financial ratios are relationships determined from a company's financial information and used for comparison purposes. You can use many different ratios depending on the nature of your business as well as what management's needs are at any time, but the following are the most widely used across a range of companies.

1. **Gross profit margin.** Derived by dividing gross profit by sales, this is the average gross profit on each dollar of sales before operating expenses. It helps work out the profitability of each product that you sell.

2. **Net profit margin.** Derived by dividing net income by sales, this is the percentage profit after operating expenses the business makes for every dollar of revenue. It's used to show whether you're making a profit after covering all your costs.

---

9 You can search an individual company's financials on the Nasdaq site. https://www.nasdaq.com/quotes/company-financials.aspx

3. **Current ratio.** Derived by dividing your current assets by your current liabilities, this helps measure the solvency of your business.

4. **Inventory turnover.** Derived by dividing the cost of goods sold by your inventory, this shows how often your stock is sold and replaced in a particular period.

5. **Return on owner's equity.** Derived by dividing net income by owner's equity compares the net business income to the equity invested in the business.

6. **Job costing.** Derived by tracking the revenue, expenses, and profit of a unique product, project, or job, including direct labor, direct materials and overhead.

Know which predictors affect your business

If you're using the assets listed on your balance sheet to tell you the actual value of your company, you could be in for a shock when you conduct a valuation. Net worth (subtracting liabilities from assets) can tell you your value right now, but it won't tell you what you'll be worth tomorrow, next week, or next year.

Some companies use their budgets to gauge success. A well-devised and controlled budget can tell the story of a company, including the schedule for adding new customers and how many, the number of employees on payroll, the plan for updating equipment, office space size, and more.

Unfortunately, the world never entirely goes according to budget, and it seldom goes to plan.

Financials, formulas, and budgets are all important to predict and track results, but it's the <u>actions</u> people take that create results, so on a regular basis, it's essential to measure the actions that lead to the results. This is the surest way we know to predict the future of a business.

Good management is about measuring outcomes to ensure that the company meets its goals. Effective managers develop Key Performance Indicators (KPIs) to measure whether team members are completing their scheduled actions every day, week, and month.

Good management measures to get numbers and to track the effects change has on them. Good managers set about improving one number at a time, and once they've improved that, they set about improving the next one. Management boils down to testing, measuring and knowing the numbers. Managers should be able to predict the future with their numbers.

If we're not hitting our numbers, we don't change our goals, we change actions. And it's the Key Performance Indicators that help us identify which actions should improve, and how. Key Performance Indicators measure a team member's results and their actions in the form of leading and lagging indicators.

Lagging indicators are typically output oriented, measured after the fact which makes them easy to measure but hard to improve or influence. Leading indicators are input oriented and measure specific activity. They can be hard to measure and easily show bias.[10] Effective business development requires understanding both.

Managers are not the only ones who should know their numbers. Everyone should. Every team member should know their numbers and be able to report on them at any time. This gives clarity regarding the impact they're having on their department and, by extension, the entire company.

Here are some typical KPIs for various areas:

Example KPIs for Marketing
Ad click-through ratio (CTR)
Average response rates of campaigns
Brand awareness percentage
Brand consideration
Brand credibility
Brand strength
Column inches of media coverage
Consumer awareness
Contact rate (number of contacts effectively contacted/ number of names in the target list)
Cost per converted lead
Cost per lead

---

10 The KPI Library site has a good definition of leading indicators. https://kpilibrary.com/topics/lag-ging-and-leading-indicators.

Example KPIs for Finance

Accounts payable amount

Accounts receivable collection period

Accounts receivable amount

Actual expenses

Amount due (per customer)

Average customer receivable

Average monetary value of invoices outstanding

Average monetary value of overdue invoices

Budget vs. actual

Invoices sent promptly

Example KPIs for Manufacturing

Asset utilization

Availability

Avoided cost

Capacity utilization

Comparative analytics for products, plants, divisions, companies

Compliance rates (for government regulations, etc.)

Quality

Customer satisfaction / Net Promoter Score

Cycle time

Example KPIs for Retail

> Average inventory
>
> Cost of goods sold
>
> Gross profit budget percentage
>
> Sales budget percentage
>
> Discounts
>
> Gross profit
>
> Leads / Customers per day
>
> Conversion rate
>
> Average dollar sale
>
> Number of transactions

Example KPIs for Accommodation and Food Services

> Average income per guest
>
> Average revenue per table
>
> Quality
>
> Labor cost per guest
>
> Minutes per table turn
>
> Profit per table

The Magic of Adding Zeros through Execution

A magic spell is based on the idea that a series of otherwise ordinary words, put into the right order, can make things happen. You just have to know which words and which order, which means that anyone without that information will fail to achieve the same effect. That's why secret societies guarded their magic words and incantations, to make sure their power didn't fall into the wrong hands … or mouths.

As you've seen in this chapter, processes use language to describe the correct order of actions that produce a consistent result. If they're kept secret from those who need them, or they don't even exist, the result is a loss of business due to inconsistent outcomes.

Performing finely-tuned processes every day in every transaction results in consistency that satisfies your constituents.

EXECUTION	
STAKEHOLDERS *Financial stability*	**TEAM MEMBERS** *Known expectations*

Stakeholders benefit from the resulting financial stability, and Team Members benefit because everyone always knows what the company expects of them.

As you saw in this chapter, the Discipline of Execution adds zeros through

- **processes** that maximize outcomes;

- **management** that guides the team to be competent and productive;

- **financial controls** that measure outcomes to ensure that the company meets its goals.

A company's processes can be one of its most valuable assets, they determine how and what it creates. If those assets don't physically exist, it's as if the business is truly creating something out of nothing, a real feat of magical thinking.

CHAPTER 11
EMOTIONAL CONNECTION:
THE LOVE POTION

ADDING ZEROS THROUGH THE DISCIPLINE OF MISSION

Why don't people like us? More specifically, why don't the people we want to like us like us as much as we like them?

Throughout history, the love potion has been a part of wishful thinking: the ability to make someone bond to you, even if they didn't want to. Especially if they didn't want to. No need to wait for fate or actual emotions: one sip and they're infatuated.

Of course, in the many stories that feature this magical concoction, there is no joy in the relationship, the would-be wooer realizes that without true desire, the relationship is an empty one.

The moral of the story is that true emotional connection can't be forced or faked. No one knows how or why it happens, but when it does it's deep and real, built on what each party perceives in the other and how it makes them feel. Not everyone feels the same way about everyone else — and that's what makes the world go round. We all have a different reason for being, and we look for something in others that can make that resonate within ourselves, even if the thing that resonates in us comes from a company instead of a person.

Every organization has a reason for being, which is the reason some people become huge fans of some companies.

A lot of companies have sincere and serious Mission Statements describing their reasons for being, but a lot of them are feel-good platitudes designed to get buy-in from as many people as possible. Who would object to the following missions?

> To build the Web's most convenient, secure, cost-effective payment solution.
> — **PayPal**

> Delight our customers, employees, and shareholders by relentlessly delivering the platform and technology advancements that become essential to the way we work and live.
> — **Intel**

> To deliver information on the people, ideas, and technologies changing the world to our community of affluent business decision makers.
> — **Forbes**

> To be a company that inspires and fulfils your curiosity.
> — **Sony**

> To be the global energy company most admired for its people, partnership, and performance.
> — **Chevron**

> To create shareholder and societal value while reducing the environmental footprint along the value chains in which we operate.
> — **DuPont**

Some of these statements, from some of the most significant companies in the world, could describe the mission of any number of good companies. We believe these statements are failures because they don't define the company's unique reason for being and offer nothing to help it achieve its goals. What do these lofty statements mean for customers? For stakeholders? For anyone? What do they even say, anyhow? For a lot of reasons, we think esoteric, future-oriented mission statements are a fad that's outlived its purpose.

This is not to say we don't believe in **mission.** The discipline of Mission is all about fostering an emotional connection between the company and people: customers,  employees, stakeholders, community members. To do this, we believe it's more appropriate to have a Purpose Statement that can answer the question anyone would ask of a company: Why do you do what you do in the here and now?

How to add zeros to Mission

You can increase emotional connection between your company and your constituents by understanding and using these three components of the Discipline of Mission:

- Core Values

- Purpose Statement

- Giving back

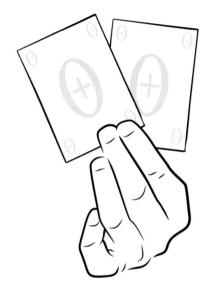

Let's look at each of these now in detail to see how they cereate an emotional connection.

CORE VALUES

Core values always exist, even if we didn't sit down and create them. They define our behaviors. Analyze the behaviors of a group, and you'll reveal its core values, the attitudes and guiding principles that govern the actions of that group's culture. And every organization has a culture, whether they openly embrace and shape its core values or not.

The core values for your organizational culture are something the company must explicitly create, lead, and manage because they determine how the employees of a company act and behave toward each other and the rest of the world. Core values also enable external audiences like customers, suppliers or investors to understand and value who the company is and for what it stands.

THIS IS IMPORTANT: Instead of aspirational or generic statements, base your core values on behaviors that are already alive in the organization. We need to be willing to hire and fire based on them.

Identify Core Values in 6 steps

Step 1. Identify the 5-12 members of your executive team who influence and impact the company. They must be committed to developing and guiding the culture of the organization.

Step 2. Hold a discussion session to brainstorm about the behaviors of current team members that you want to see everyone imitate; you might come up with dozens of behaviors observed in 5 to 50 people. Make sure you're describing specific actions ("tells the truth") rather than vague adjectives ("honest").

Step 3. Make a list that describes each of the desired behaviors from Step 2, using behavior-based phrases, such as "communicates orally in a well-organized, courteous, and effective manner," so people know what the company culture expects from them.

Step 4. Sort the list of behaviors by topic, aiming for a set of six to eight themes.

Step 5. Select a word or short phrase to define each behavioral value, then create a short sentence that names them in terms that are meaningful to your organization. Each phrase is a core value that describes the company's desired culture, such as: "We make decisions based on our values and our goals."

Step 6. Implement core values. Train, communicate, and reinforce these core values in daily practices.

Examples of Core Values

We believe that Zappos' 10 Core Values are exemplary.[1] They simply state the desired behavior and then give a detailed explanation of what that means and what is expected. Any team member at any level or length of service can learn and review the company's culture.

---

1 Zappos lays out clearly its approach on itss website, Zappos Insights. https://www.zapposinsights.com/about/core-.values?gclid=Cj0KCQiAh_DTBRCTARIsABlT9MbF42XqCgwwzvHHp0jXIeONRyzxLW-TIvwsrIwe L30KO4PqXolqLbcUaApdOEALw_wcB

Deliver WOW Through Service – WOW is such a
short, simple word, but it really encompasses a lot of
things. To WOW, you must differentiate yourself, which
means doing something a little unconventional and
innovative. You must do something that's above and
beyond what's expected. And whatever you do must
have an emotional impact on the receiver. We are not
an average company, our service is not average, and we
don't want our people to be average. We expect every
employee to deliver WOW.

Embrace and Drive Change – Change is constant,
which is why we shouldn't ever fear it, but to also
embrace it enthusiastically, and perhaps even more
importantly, to encourage and drive it. We must always
plan for and be prepared for constant change. Don't

be satisfied with the status quo because historically, the companies that get into trouble are the ones who aren't able to adapt with the times.

Create Fun and a Little Weirdness – One way that we differ from other companies is that we're not afraid to be a little weird. Weird certainly isn't a bad thing – it can be fun! One of the reasons why our company culture is so successful is because our atmosphere is fun, and employees are never afraid to be themselves.

Be Adventurous, Creative, and Open-Minded – While you never want to be reckless, it's important to take risks and embrace your creativity. You may end up making mistakes, but if you don't make any mistakes, that only means that you haven't taken any risks. We don't want to be complacent and accept the status quo – we want to aim for more.

Pursue Growth and Learning – We believe that everyone should be constantly trying to grow from a personal and a professional standpoint. By pushing our employees to unlock their full potential, we'll help them achieve a greater level of fulfillment.

Build Open and Honest Relationships with Communication – We strive to create strong relationships between all our members so that everyone feels comfortable to contribute in every way they can. This allows us to have a diversity of ideas, opinions, and viewpoints that give us a better chance of succeeding and making a positive impact as a company.

Build a Positive Team and Family Spirit – At Zappos, our team is our family, which is why we place such an emphasis on having a positive company culture. Team members always have a direct influence on one another, which is why we aim to foster an environment that produces positivity.

Do More with Less – By doing more with less, we mean that there's always room for improvements. We believe in hard work and dedication to stay ahead of the competition (or would-be competition).

Be Passionate and Determined – Passion is the fuel that will drive us and our companies forward. We're inspired to accomplish what we're doing because we believe in it. We don't take no for an answer, because if we did, we wouldn't be here as a company today.

Be Humble – Lastly, while we've grown tremendously as a company, we've learned to take nothing for granted. There always are challenges that lie ahead and nothing in life is a certainty. It's important to stay humble, carry ourselves with a quiet confidence, and treat others the same way that we want to be treated.

Six Ways to Implement Core Values

When you've identified your core values, you'll be able to live by them every day and implement them into the aspects of the company where they'll have the most impact on your culture.

1. **Making decisions.** When facing difficult decisions, use core values to evaluate options to ensure you'll support and model them so others will watch and learn from you.

2. **Hiring.** Use your core values when interviewing to determine if applicants fit the culture of the company. When personal values match corporate values, the new hire tends to live the brand and be a great employee.

3.   **Performance evaluations.** Use your core values when reviewing an individual's work-related performance, so that pay increases take into account how well they live the values.

4.   **Feedback.** When providing developmental feedback and kudos, share how well people are living the core values.

5.   **Personal development planning.** When creating individual development plans, identify one or two core values the employee should enhance or improve during the next 90-day period, who will do what, and what behaviors will grow.

6.   **Firing.** Use core values as a basis for firing someone who, after getting training and feedback and having them included in their personal development plans, isn't willing to live by them.

PURPOSE STATEMENT

We're not alone on this planet. Much as we might like to think we're unique, we're more like other people than we're different from them. That's not to say we're the same as everybody, of course, but we do share our passions, beliefs, and values with other people. According to Jason Burnham, Principal at **Experience Innovation Strativity Group Inc.**, of Hackensack, NJ, this is how we find common purpose.

Knowing our purpose in the world helps us answer the why question: why are we here? Burnham believes a person can answer that by leveraging their skills and aligning their needs, values, and aspirations with the impact they want to have on the world. [2]

Businesses also want to have an impact on the world, so leaders should use the power of shared purpose to create an emotional connection to every person in their organizations. Purposeful leaders leverage their common purpose to inspire, unify, and drive collective action to achieve goals. Purpose-driven brands produce business sustainability and positively impact the world by identifying a purpose common to their stakeholders and customers, and to society at large.

---

2 Jason Burnham, "What Is Your 'Why'?" How I Learned to Live My Purpose, Sustainable Brands, August 31, 2015.

A purpose statement tells people what ignites your passion and inspires you to be the best you can be. It draws on skills and experience while stimulating personal growth and future opportunity.

The single question that can unlock your company's purpose is this: What is your organization here to do, besides make money?

The Thing About Money

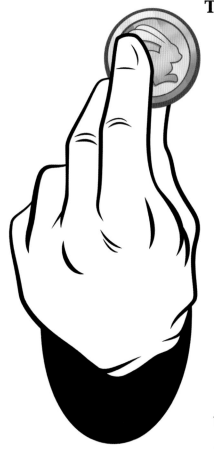

Part of leadership is giving people something to be passionate about; a common purpose that gets them excited when they show up for work because they can see that they are doing something of value for themselves and the broader community, every single day. It's challenging to feel passionate about a company that's only focused on making money.

That might seem to fly in the face of the truth, many people are passionate about money. Everyone wants it, and when they get it, they want still more. It motivates a lot of people to do a lot of things.

But money is only a short-term motivator.

Once there's enough of it to satisfy basic needs or dreams of riches, (most) people need more to inspire them to work so hard. They look for passion. This applies equally to employees and members of the executive team. It's likely that you're doing what you're currently doing for a living because it's about more than money. It's more likely about your purpose.

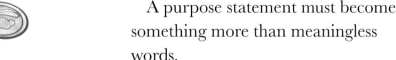

Making money is the fringe benefit of fulfilling your purpose. When you fulfill your purpose, money flows. When organizations achieve their purpose, adding zeros flows. When you don't know what your purpose is, there can be money problems and worse.

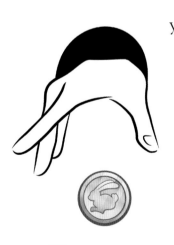

When you have a clear purpose, you'll change the world and all the people and communities with whom your organization interacts. When your entire team believes there's a compelling reason for you to be in business, there's an emotional connection with the organization that motivates and inspires them even when they have frustrations.

A purpose statement must become something more than meaningless words.

A company must live its purpose with appropriate actions. Southwest Airlines' stated purpose is "to connect people to what's important in their lives through friendly, reliable, and low-cost air travel." This statement has kept it from charging customers for checked bags. The company would reap immediate profits by doing so, but that would betray its purpose. Southwest differentiates itself and demonstrates its commitment to that purpose in its national advertising campaign, Bags Fly Free.[3]

Here are some examples of purpose statements:

Empowering people to stay a step ahead in life and in business. — **ING**

Nourishing families so they can flourish and thrive. — **Kellogg**

To help people manage risk and recover from the hardship of unexpected loss. — **IAG**

3 Nate Dvorak and Bryan Ott ,"A Company's Purpose Has to Be a Lot More than Words," Business Journal, July 28, 2015. http://news.gallup.com/businessjournal/184376/company-purpose-lot-words.aspx.

GE people worldwide are dedicated to turning imaginative ideas into leading products and services that help solve some of the world's toughest problems. — **GE**

Delivering Happiness. — **Zappos**

Google Inc. was founded to make it easier to find high-quality information on the web. — **Google**

Wikipedia is a collaborative project to produce a free and complete encyclopedia in every language. — **Wikipedia**

With great courage, integrity, and love — we embrace our responsibility to co-create a world where each of us, our communities, and our planet can flourish. All the while, celebrating the sheer love and joy of food. — **Whole Foods Market**

Improving Lives — **TOMS**

GIVING BACK

Let's talk about the work-life balance advocated by many business leaders. It calls for living two separate lives, one filled with passion, one focused on making money,

as if people had dual personalities, split down the middle. Who can live like that? It's no wonder organizations are having trouble establishing emotional connections with their employees or the community.

That's why we think the work-life balance idea is a mistake. Ideally, your personal and business lives should not be separated, but integrated, getting rid of the need for balance. When we are truly living our company's purpose, business and personal life merge and become one, and in that there is balance.

A company supports its community in ways much more powerful than an individual could by acting alone. The organization gives to charities, spearheads civic projects, and enables the team to volunteer in the community. The company amplifies the individual's efforts, rewarding him or her for joining a common purpose with others. When an employee's purpose aligns with the organization's purpose, they are more motivated, more creative, more productive, and more satisfied. When team members think of their work as part of their lives, they can fulfill their purpose and add value to their community through that work.

We can think of no finer example of a company that lives its purpose by giving back than TOMS. It is a shoe company that makes people want to work for them, invest in them, and buy their shoes. Its purpose statement could be summed up as improving lives, and it exists to fulfill that purpose.

While traveling in Argentina in 2006, TOMS Founder Blake Mycoskie witnessed the hardships faced by children growing up without shoes. Wanting to help, he created TOMS, a shoe company that would match every pair of shoes purchased with a new pair of shoes for a child in need. What began as a simple idea has evolved into a powerful business model that helps address need and advance health, education, and economic opportunity for children and their communities around the world. TOMS One for One Program uses the proceeds from its shoe sales to provide shoes, sight, water, safe birth, and kindness (bullying prevention services) to people in need.

Importantly, TOMS measures the impact of its giving and can track the results of its giving back. For example, TOMS philanthropy is responsible for:

- 700+ jobs supported by TOMS Giving Shoe production;

- 4 countries where 10 different styles of Giving Shoes are produced;

- 20+ companies with a social mission provided with start-up funds by TOMS;

- 100% of TOMS coffee is sustainably sourced;

- Over 2 million children have been protected from hookworm with medication and TOMS Shoes provided by our Giving Partners;

- 42% increase in maternal health care program participation as a result of shoe distribution;

- an increase in student enrollment of 1000 in Liberian primary school classrooms after TOMS Shoe distribution began;

- 100 children identified during shoe-integrated health screenings as needing malnutrition care in Malawi;

- vision restored to 500,000 people in need.

TOMS[4] also makes it clear that it's their customers who are responsible for this change in the world change, telling them that their purchases support economic opportunity, gender equality, access to education, and restored independence.

There is no better example of the difference between mission statement and real purpose than TOMS success. In our opinion, this is what business is about - making the world a better place by adding zeros through impact that can be measured using KPIs, just like any other business output.

4 www.toms.com/improving-lives

We think it's important to get emotional sustenance where we work, in the things we do every day, and in the things we do to make our world a better place. Those emotional connections come from fulfilling our purpose, living our core values, and giving back to make the world a better place.

These "deep" concepts articulate why you give back to your community as an organization and as an individual. When you give to your community, you get something in return, the satisfaction of knowing your actions have made a difference to people in the local and global communities. The organization also gets something in return for using their business skills to improve their communities and making them stronger: goodwill from neighbors and consumers that leads to substantial feedback, referrals, and customer retention.

Business leaders — specifically the executive team — have an obligation to give their time and resources to those less fortunate, thereby setting an example for the rest of the team. We do better as an organization by doing good in the community.

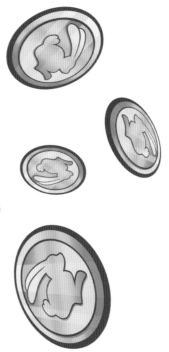

The organization also gets something in return for using their business skills to improve their communities and making them stronger: goodwill from neighbors and consumers that leads to substantial feedback, referrals, and customer retention.

Business leaders — specifically the executive team — have an obligation to give their time and resources to those less fortunate, thereby setting an example for the rest of the team. We do better as an organization by doing good in the community.

THE MAGIC OF ADDING ZEROS THROUGH MISSION

Love potions are supposed to override the natural reactions a person may have toward another, forcing them to feel deeply about someone they otherwise have no feelings for. It's based on an idea that emotional connections are superficial feelings that can be manipulated, and that such manipulations are preferable to working to become a person worthy of someone's attention, respect, and love.

Being everything to everybody might seem like a good way to be attractive to a broad demographic, but beauty is only skin-deep. Those attracted to the shiny and new will soon move on to the next thing; those looking for meaningful relationships aren't interested once they see past the veneer.

As you've seen in this chapter, the strong emotional connections that exist between a company and the people who interact with it and that result from the company's work ethic and values have real benefits for constituents.

MISSION	
Community *sustenance*	**Stakeholders** *amplification of purpose*

The Community benefits because those connections sustain the community itself, and the Stakeholders benefit because their ability to change the world is amplified.

As you saw in this chapter, the Discipline of Mission adds zeros through

- **core values** that govern the actions of the organization's culture;

- **purpose statements** that inspire, unify, and drive collective action to achieve goals;

- **giving back** to improve communities and make them stronger.

A company's mission is broader than a calculated formula — a love potion — stating why its customers should love it. A company's mission is the purpose that it lives every day, that gives us energy and gives us desire. Emotional connections are built by sharing that purpose, helping us feel that we're not alone in the world because we're working together to make it better here and now. That is a company's mission.

PART 4: PRACTICE, PRACTICE, PRACTICE

In theory, magic is wonderful: wave a wand, say a few words, and alacazam! an audience is wowed.

In practice, magic takes a lot of practice. Lots and lots. Magicians practice coin and card manipulation for hundreds, if not thousands, of hours, just to get to the point where it's a habit they can rely on. They study themselves in mirrors to pinpoint flaws and identify areas that need work. They know that, once a skill has the muscle memory of habit, it can become the foundation for ideas that will wow an audience. Without that foundational habit, phenomenal illusions like *The Miser's Dream* just aren't possible. No audience will wait around for the big finale if they see coins falling out of hidden pockets and rolling along the floor.

Exponential growth also takes regular practice and review to produce the magic that wows customers. That's what strategic thinking is: the process we follow so the audience sees magic and not the strings and mirrors. Execution planning is the rehearsal of that process, refining it so it's ready for opening night, when the Big Hairy Audacious Goal has its premier and astonishes the crowds.

Let's get to work!

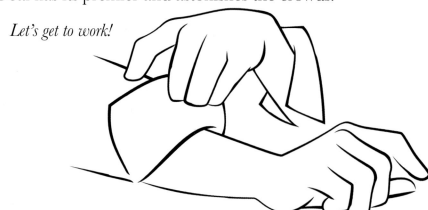

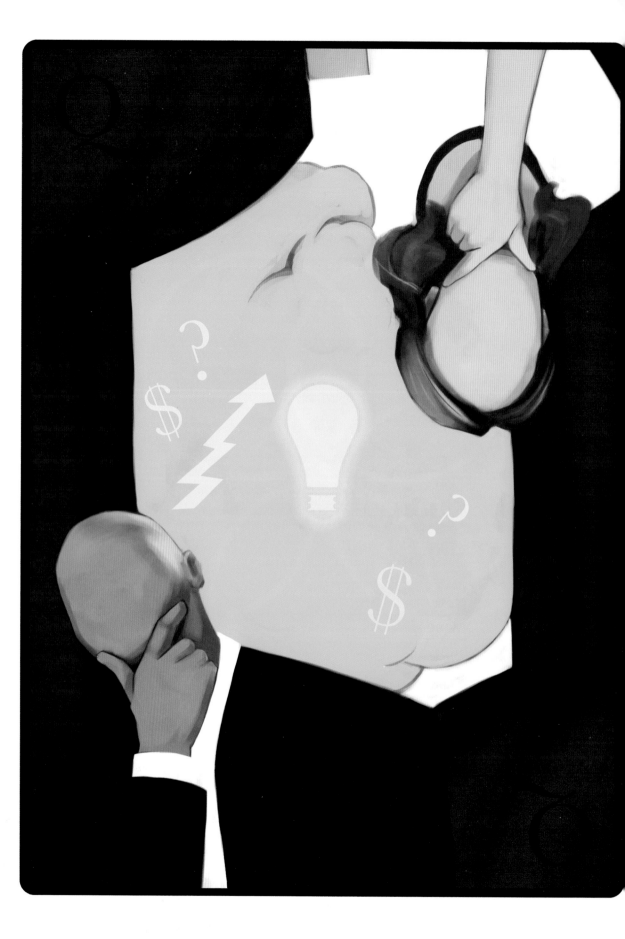

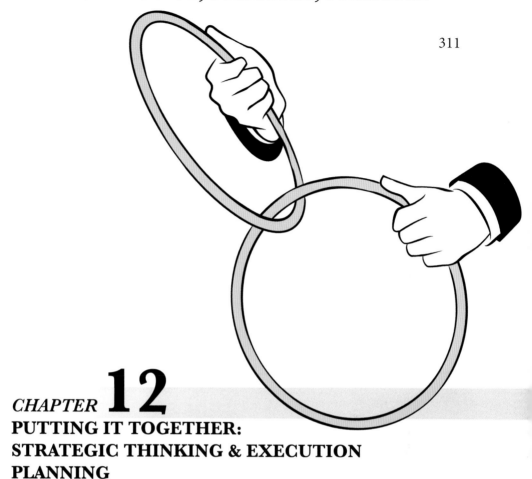

CHAPTER **12**
PUTTING IT TOGETHER:
STRATEGIC THINKING & EXECUTION
PLANNING

Too often the focus in business is on strategic planning without paying attention to how that plan becomes a reality. The planning really needs to be about how to execute the strategies you develop. You need to have short-term execution plans that carry out your strategies for adding zeros to the 5 Disciplines. This means that everyone needs to be on the same page and everyone knows who is doing what.

To achieve this, senior management needs to dive deep into the business every year and focus on the alignment of the organization.

These deep - dives are conversations to ensure that we understand different viewpoints, we understand our own business, and we understand the market. The result is long-term strategic decisions for the business: clear next-steps of **who's** doing **what** by **when.**

The hardest thing in business is to stand by our decisions.

Once we've decided to go down a path, our actions must support that choice. We chose that path based on our knowledge and expertise, and the world doesn't always behave in the manner we predicted. But we must stick to our guns and the pro-active course of action we know is correct. If we're reactive and start changing things around, we'll never know what created a problem or what solved it.

Senior management must commit to the strategic thinking and execution planning process and commit to the time it takes, realizing that this process is about the discussion and making decisions that lead to agreement about the company's alignment.

Let's look at how to make that happen.

ANNUAL AND QUARTERLY SESSIONS

The discussions that lead to decision-making need to happen on a regular basis. There should be an annual deep-dive session (sometimes called a retreat) where the company engages in a process that leads to the resolutions and directions that add zeros to the company. There should also be quarterly Action Planning sessions for coming up with the specific tasks and metrics that add those zeros and measure their impact.

Who should be there?

Strategic thinking session activities are for the business's senior management team.

If your business doesn't have a management team you need to assign one. An important management function is to have each member of senior management responsible for understanding how the business is satisfying each constituent group. For example, the person responsible for community interaction, usually the CEO, needs to have a good understanding of how the community's viewing the company.

The purpose of the senior manager is to understand what's going on in a department, in the customer's experience in the world. Before they come to the meeting, the people in charge of each department need to get input from their teams, a consensus or an idea of what's happening so they can report to the group. These responsibilities can overlap, and multiple people can be involved. The Sales Manager and Marketing Manager will have their perspectives of how the customer sees the company. Senior management needs to balance that understanding with the company's strategy.

The Need for an Abundance Mentality

Obviously, to chart the future direction of your company, you need abundance thinking. The first reaction to new ideas shouldn't be no, but what if? You need wide-ranging, frank discussions that are open to information from every source, accepting that no one knows everything.

Make sure everyone is personally invested in the outcome of the process and is a knowledgeable and clear, creative thinker who exhibits an Abundance Mindset in the following ways:

Thinking Big versus Thinking Small. People with the Abundant Mentality are known for creating Big, Hairy Audacious Goals — it becomes part of their DNA — while the Scarcity Mindset is all about limits.

Plenty versus Lack. Because the Abundance Mentality sees that there is plenty of everything in the world, from resources, love, relationships, wealth and opportunities, they know they can afford what they want in life and say I can afford that ... instead of automatically believing I can't afford that, even when it's not true.

Happiness versus Resentment. A person with an Abundance Mentality is a happy optimist, genuinely happy for others' success, while someone with a Scarcity Mindset is bitter and competitive, seeing the success of others as taking away from themselves.

Embracing Change versus Fear of Change. People with an Abundance Mentality embrace and accept change as an integral part of life, even if it's challenging or difficult to navigate. Those with a Scarcity Mindset are plagued by fear, complaining about and resisting change of any kind.

Proactive versus Reactive. Those with an Abundance Mentality take a pro-active approach to life, strategically planning for the future. People with a Scarcity Mindset are passive, waiting for things to happen to them.

Learning versus Knowing It All. People with an Abundance Mentality have a never-ending thirst for knowledge and developing new skills: they crave learning and growth. Those with the Scarcity Mindset believe they already know everything worth knowing ... even when contradicted by facts.

What Is Working versus What Is Not Working.
Those with an Abundance Mentality have a daily focus on what's working? The person with the Scarcity Mindset adopts a victim mentality, choosing to focus on what they perceive to be failing, often snatching defeat from the jaws of victory. It is nearly impossible to plan for the future with this kind of thinking. Avoid it if possible.

When should You Hold the Session?

Thinking strategically is not a once-a-year event. It's a constant approach to execution planning. If you've never done this before, you need to do a strategic thinking session as soon as possible, followed by a deep-dive every year.

Every 90 days, you'll revisit and reassess the effects of the zeros you're adding and whether you're achieving your priorities and goals. You'll update your quarterly action plans to reflect your findings.

Deep Dives: immediately [if never before] and then annually.

Quarterlies: every 90 days.

Where Should You Hold the Session?

Ideally, the Annual session is two days long, held off-site to remove all distractions from the job at hand and enable deep work.

Deep work is the ability to focus without distraction on a cognitively demanding task. It's a skill that allows you to quickly master complicated information and produce better results in less time and generate high-level output while leveraging expertise. Deep work is becoming increasingly rare in our attention economy where there's an ever-growing number of distractions. Unless your talent and skills absolutely dwarf those of your competition, the deep workers among them will out-produce you.

To optimize your performance, it's important to enforce strict isolation until you've completed the task at hand. This leverages the following law of productivity: (Time Spent) x (Intensity of Focus) = High-Quality Work Produced.

As Stephen Covey describes it in *7 Habits of Highly Effective People,* this is work that is Important and Not Urgent, and rarely gets the attention it needs when anything seemingly urgent is on the horizon. Therefore, there should be no day-to-day distractions like email, phone calls, office responsibilities and activities, or other demands on participants' time.

Providing live-in accommodation for the session is useful, so participants can go to their private rooms when needed for off-stage time. It's nice to have other spaces where people can retreat as necessary to get out of each other's hair or take a break. Having a kitchen where food can be obtained whenever it's needed also enables the group to have time at the end of the day to eat together. This is invaluable in creating bonding experiences that lead to dynamic work sessions. Secluded retreats, game parks, conservation park conference facilities, and five-star hotels are excellent venues.

A SAMPLE AGENDA FOR ANNUAL AND QUARTERLY SESSIONS

Whether you engage a facilitator or lead the session yourself, a typical deep-dive strategic thinking session might consist of the following main activities. This is not a hard-and-fast agenda, but a listing of what we feel are key points for discussion. You should feel free to alter it to suit your needs and circumstances.

STEP 1. Annually. Discuss the Current Strategy

A. Review how the company currently fulfills the four characteristics of a good strategy:

i. Opportunity

- How is the company responding to existing opportunities in the market?

- What can it do to capitalize on any future opportunities?

- What can it do to capitalize on opportunities that it isn't dealing well with at present?

ii. Scalability

- How is the company expanding in the market place?

- How is it growing?

- Are all the aspects of scalability suitably addressed, and if not, what can or needs to be done?

iii. Leverageability

- Is the company making full use of leverage?
- If not, what can be done?
- Are there any untapped leverage opportunities that should be addressed?

iv. Marketability

- Does the company have access to the right markets?
- Are there additional markets that it should be participating in?
- Do target audiences have sufficient understanding of all the company's products and services?
- Define the company's strategy in a sentence. A good one-sentence strategy indicates how the company is going to win will make the following sections about setting goals more focused and much easier.
- If you've done this in a previous session, take the time to review it. How are we fulfilling it? Does everyone know how we will win?

STEP 2. Annually. Reflect on the previous year.

Identify the successes of the last year. What worked? What were the results? What made those successes happen? What did you learn last year? What didn't go the way you wanted? What do you need to do differently? What don't you want to experience again? As you reflect, make connections to how your successes link to the abundant mentality.

STEP 3. Annually and Quarterly. Review the current state of the business.

Here you should review documents and information to bring everyone up to date on the company's statistics, including full details of the products sold and the market that exists for them, annual revenue, profit, cash flow, market share and other pertinent details. Managers should make sure they have all the information they need reported from their teams so they're fully prepared.

A. Examine current trends.

Discuss trends within your industry, the operating environment of your company and the internal situation within it. What effect is the state of the economy having on your industry? Are customers loyal, restless, fleeing, growing? How is all of this trending?

What caliber of staff will be required to allow you to reach future targets or goals? Will those people be readily available? Where will you find them? How much will they cost?

B. Examine pertinent industry facts in detail.

Is new technology beginning to make itself felt? Is new technology needed?

C. Examine your assumptions.

At this stage of the process, you'll have made assumptions based on your discussions about what your future may hold. These include suppositions about your competitors, the needs of your market, the trends you see coming, and other information you have. While your assumptions give you a lens through which to view the future, remember that they are not necessarily based on facts.

D. *Annually only* Conduct a SWOT analysis.

Here, as a group, you want to draw up four different lists: the business's Strengths, Weaknesses,

Opportunities, and Threats for the time period under discussion. Strengths and weaknesses relate to your organization internally; opportunities and threats relate to external factors. Addressing weaknesses, taking advantage of strengths, making use of opportunities, and managing real or perceived threats enables you to determine the areas of the company where it could be smart and/or critical to add zeros. A diversity of viewpoints is crucial, others may see things you're blind to.

Identify the top two or three that you will deal with in the coming year. This is the beginning of your action plan.

STEP 4. Annually and Quarterly.

Review the 5 Disciplines and Your Constituents' Satisfaction

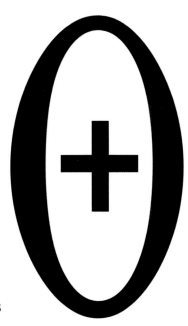

Chances are your organization didn't score 100% in the assessment you took in Chapter 6. Some Disciplines are going great guns while others need attention to satisfy the constituents associated with them.

It's tempting to look at the discipline with the lowest score, but that doesn't necessarily mean it's the one to pay attention to right now.

Instead, focus on the change that can make the biggest difference across the board. To find it, consider the constituent group you believe is the least satisfied. Look at the two disciplines that affect that group:

Stakeholders are affected by Mission & Execution.

Teams are affected by Execution & People.

Customers are affected by People & Business Development.

The Company is affected by Business Development & Strategy.

The Community is affected by Strategy & Mission.

If, for example, you identify the Community as your least satisfied constituency, it means the Discipline of Strategy or the Discipline of Mission is an area of concern. How did these fare in your assessment? Discuss how and where you could add zeros to these disciplines. Which zeros would make the biggest difference?

It's likely that more than one constituent group needs attention. That's to be expected, few organizations are adding zeros in all the places they're needed. Consider the disciplines that affect the other group. Ultimately, though, work on your most critical issues first, focusing on those that, when corrected, will touch 10 other things and cause them to improve.

STEP 5. Annually. Visualize the future

Now you know where you are today. You know which disciplines you need to work on, where you can add zeros, and the things you can change to make things better in the present. What will you do with this information?

Jim Collins, in his book Good to Great, talks about the need to identify one Big Hairy Audacious Goal (BHAG) to force you to think bigger and differently. Your BHAG should be so B, H and A that you don't have a clue as to how you'll achieve it or if it's even possible. You want and need to think that big to push yourself into the realm of exponential growth, which is in and of itself a BHAG .

A. First, Set Your Big, Hairy, Audacious Goal (BHAG®)

Answer this: Where do you want to be in 10 years? What kind of exponential growth can you dare to dream about?

Don't think this makes sense? Well, Microsoft had a BHAG of having a computer on every desk running their software and look what that did for them!

B. Set priorities

Once you've set your BHAG, set your priorities, the three to five things that you must get right in that 10 - year period to achieve your BHAG. This is where you can truly add zeros. Review the 5 Disciplines and how you're satisfying your constituents to help you set your priorities.

A priority is defined up front, and it's satisfied when the senior management team agrees it is. The clarity of each priority and the measurement of its success is their judgment call. It could be that there are three priorities, and 2 of them are measurable, like whether the company gains 100,000 new customers. The third could be we have excellent relationships with the community. Success in that case can be determined by simply saying, "our priority was X. Do we all agree we achieved that?" Note that while the 10 - year BHAG priorities are very broad, subsequent priorities require detail.

The point of any priority is to serve as a road map for the company so that if anyone veers off course from any of the priorities, they should be challenged about how they're using their time.

Once you've set priorities, identify three to five measurable outcomes that will tell you whether you're achieving your BHAG. This could be the number of sales you make over a stated period, the average sale amount, frequency of return customers, etc.

SET A BIG HAIRY AUDACIOUS GOAL (BHAG)
Identify 3-5 priorities for the next 10 years
Define targets for measuring success

Some of these measures, known as Key Performance Indicators (KPIs), may not even exist right now, but they will. You'll create them as part of the overall plan. That's why you're thinking courageously and freely right now. Remember: the abundance mentality is the name of the game.

Set three-year goals. Staring down a 10-year goal can be daunting, so to make it manageable, break it into 3-year chunks. To achieve those three-year goals, what are the three to five priorities you must get right in that 3-year period? Three-year priorities are more detailed than those for the BHAG ®, so use all the thinking you've engaged in so far to figure out where you choose to be at the end of each 3-year period. Define financial targets for revenue, profit, market share, and other metrics, and define non-financial targets, such as staff size, location, markets, and product mix.

Identify owners for the priorities. Priorities at these stages need owners: a person who is responsible for monitoring its progress, its actions, and its success. One person may be responsible for several priorities, but each priority has only one owner. This is especially important when you get to one-year and quarterly priorities because they need close monitoring to ensure they are on track.

Set one-year goals. Once three-year goals and priorities are sorted, you chunk them down into smaller and more immediate goals and priorities, focusing on the next 12 months.

SET 3-YEAR GOAL TOWARD ACHIEVING BHAG
Identify 3-5 priorities, each with a specific owner
Define target metrics for measuring success

Review those three-year priorities and make them more specific for the one-year timeframe. To achieve your one-year goal, what are the three to five things you must get right in that 1-year period? One-year priorities are more specific than 3-year priorities.

Define the one-year results you'll need for your financial targets to be met: again, revenue, profit, market share, etc.

SET 1-YEAR GOAL TOWARD ACHIEVING 3-YEAR GOAL
Identify 3-5 priorities for the next year
Define target metrics for measuring success

C. Create actions plans

From here, you'll develop the various actions and steps required to achieve your 1-year goals, but this happens quarterly. Here's a quick look at what that would look like, now that you know the drill:

90-DAY PLAN FOR ACHIEVING 1-YEAR GOAL
3-5 priorities for the Quarter
Actions to achieve those priorities
Target metrics for success

Quarterly priorities are extremely specific so there can be no question as to what needs to be accomplished. Note that this is the first time there are specific actions for achieving goals, and the measures of success will be quantifiable in some way.

STEP 6. Annually and quarterly. Communicate the plan

Once the goals and actions steps are defined, they must be communicated throughout the organization so everyone knows how they play a part in the company's future direction by learning what is expected of them and when.

HOW SETTING GOALS WORKS IN PRACTICE.

Sometimes it's easier to understand the various mechanics with a chart:

ANNUALLY

1. The organization sets a long-term Big Hairy Audacious Goal (BHAG) for 10 years out or more, along with the 3-5 priorities or areas they must get right to achieve the BHAG.

   For example, if the BHAG were, "Reach $500 million in annual sales," one such priority could be, "We will expand and leverage our database."

2. The organization then sets specific 3-year goals that will help them align and set direction to achieve the BHAG. Management also identifies the 3-5 priorities or areas they must get right to achieve the 3-year goals. The 3-year priorities should be linked to the BHAG priorities.

   For example, if a 3-year goal were: "Increase our database from 100,000 to 300,000," a corresponding priority could be to "develop effective data-capture strategies for customer information."

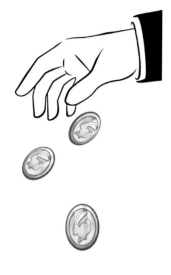

3. The organization then sets specific 1-year goals that will help them align and set direction to achieve their 3-year goals. Management also identifies the 3-5 priorities or areas they must get right to achieve the 1-year goals. Management should provide a clear written definition of what constitutes success for each priority, and a management team member should be named as the owner of each priority with the responsibility of accomplishing that priority.

For example, if a 1-year goal were "Increase our database from 100,000 to 175,000" (as a step toward achieving the matching 3-year goal in the example in #2, above), a corresponding priority could be: "Identify and target new markets in order to expand our database."

Success for this priority could be defined as: "We're focused on no fewer than three target markets, with the first in place by March 1."

Monica, the VP of Sales, is responsible for this priority.

Quarterly

1. Every quarter, the organization sets **90-day goals**, along with the **3-5 priorities** or areas that they must get right to achieve the desired quarterly results. Each priority gets a clear written description of what constitutes success for that priority and a single person at the management level is assigned to be its owner.

   Then, based on the organization's 90-day goals, each department sets its own 90-day goals that support those set by the company. Each department also sets 3-5 priorities or areas that they must get right to achieve the company's desired quarterly results. Each departmental priority gets a clear **written description of what constitutes its success,** and the department identifies a single person as the owner of each priority.

   Each department's goals and priorities should support the organization's quarterly goals.

2. <u>Each management team member</u> then creates their individual 90-day action plan that defines what they will do by when to achieve the 90-day goals and appropriate priorities. This 90-day action plan will be a roadmap for their work, decisions, timing, and results.

Ideally, everyone in the organization has a 90-day action plan that supports the quarterly goals and priorities.

3. <u>Each person</u> shares their 90-day action plan with their team members for consistency and peer review.

The point of all this planning is to assemble action plans that ensure you achieve the priorities and goals you've identified.

It's a funnel that leads from deep work to specific actions. It's broadest at the 10-year BHAG level and narrows until it reaches the 90-day quarterly level.

It looks like this:

BIG HAIRY AUDACIOUS GOAL (BHAG)
3-5 priorities for the next 10 years
Targets for success

3-YEAR GOAL TOWARD ACHIEVING BHAG
3-5 priorities for the next 3 years
Targets for success

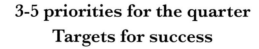

SET 1-YEAR GOAL TOWARD ACHIEVING 3-YEAR GOAL
3-5 priorities for the next year
Targets for success

90-DAY PLANS TOWARD ACHIEVING 1-YEAR GOAL
3-5 priorities for the quarter
Targets for success

At the end of each period (quarters, years, 3-year chunks), the process is revisited and reassessed to keep the organization moving toward its BHAG.

GETTING SESSION HELP FROM COACHES AND FACILITATORS

Okay, you've got the location set up, the time set aside, everyone's prepped and ready to go.

Just one thing: how do you lead a strategic session?

It's possible to lead a session by yourself, but it's challenging.

Very challenging.

Companies on the path to exponential growth often find that everything about the business grows, including problems and issues. This can lead many executives to back away from their end goals and retreat into the scarcity mentality - We're trying to do too much! These are the growing pains of changing from one state of being to another. It can be hard to recognize and break old habits while building new ones without guidance.

Best practice is having a facilitator or coach lead the quarterly planning sessions to ensure you follow the process. They keep you focused on your ultimate goals, even if the going sometimes gets tough.

As a third party, a facilitator or coach can sidestep power dynamics and ensure that everyone participates with no one dominating the discussion. Most importantly, they are skilled in leading the group through the steps necessary to identify issues and goals and collaborate on devising the action steps and timelines necessary to achieve those goals.

A qualified executive coach can add benefit by guiding the business through the process and holding executives accountable, keeping executives focused on end goals even as they deal with the daily minutia of running the business.

And not just the executives, the whole team must develop its accountability/abundance mentality, because even a single employee stuck in the trap of the scarcity mentality can scuttle progress.

The facilitator ensures participation, teaches, challenges actions, beliefs and behaviors, and allows senior management to fully participate in the session without being distracted by the tasks required to run it.

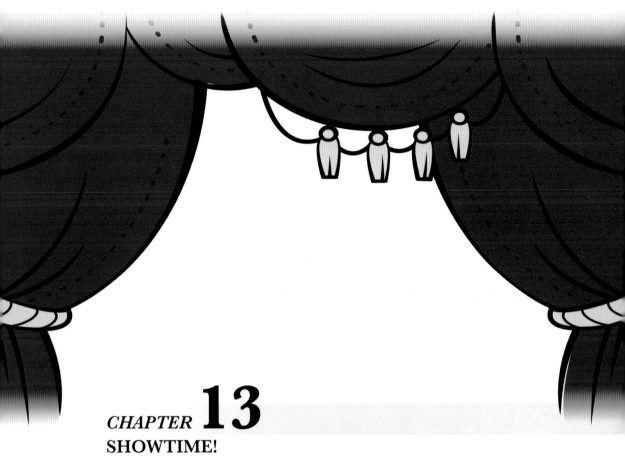

CHAPTER **13**
SHOWTIME!

As coaches, we've worked with thousands of companies to get them on the path of exponential growth. Over time, we've seen a disturbing pattern emerge: a business's profit becomes more important than its success. The companies we work with mean so much more than just money to the people who rely on them, and we've recognized that the real bottom line for a business is being sustainable, predictable, stable, and consistent so it can continue to create emotional connections between the work it does and the people it serves.

When a company only thinks of profits, it ignores hundreds, thousands, and even millions of small things that it thinks are valueless, things like morale, employee engagement, employee retention, and its impact on our communities and the world at large. But these are the things that make us want to go into work every day, make us want to do our very best, and satisfy us at the end of the day. If we're not accomplishing all of this, why run a business at all?

We believe the main point of running a business so it can achieve exponential growth is not only to increase the money in our pockets but to amplify the good it makes possible. A business is an engine of change and it enables our purpose in life. A lofty ambition? Perhaps. But it's the one that gets us up every morning, ready to do more.

We've carefully chosen to compare this attitude to magic for several reasons, but possibly the biggest is that magic, whether in fairy tales or on stage, offers us a vision of a world that's better than the one we live in, one we all wish was true. Our experience in making companies successful has shown us that those visions can be made real. When that's done with habitual intentionality so that it seems to take no effort at all, well … that's magical.

We think business should be magical by design, creating situations where it's easier to believe in enchantment than all the painstaking work and intricate details that go into wowing constituents. As you've seen in this book, true magic means no one suspects how much hard work goes into developing the necessary processes so that a skilled team can be in the right place at the right time without wasting a single motion, so it all looks natural and the audience never notices what's happening behind the scenes.

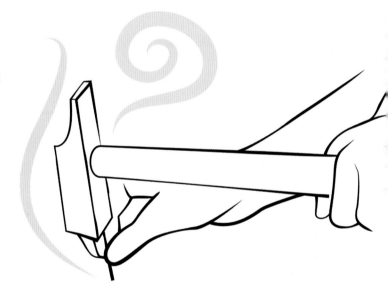

The harder the team works behind the scenes toward the shared goal of wowing their audience of constituents, the more successful they become because it's easier to believe in magic than in the labor it takes to make something look effortless. Steve Jobs's showmanship concealed a lot of very hard work that combined the business disciplines found in any company into a single integrated idea designed to astonish audiences and get them to believe in a world made better by Apple products.

The Apple experience is a magic show, and it achieves that by accepting that magic isn't real: it's really hard work to add zeros to the mess of modern commerce with all its technology, practice, planning, and support. And yet, every added zero contributes to the company's exponential growth and phenomenal success.

We wrote this book because we know you can do that, too. When a company commits to exponential growth by making even a modest investment in itself, it can achieve optimal success, because each zero-added investment multiplies the value of other such improvements.

If every aspect of your business — team morale, revenue, margins, customer loyalty, sales, everything — had a zero added to it, you'd increase its value and make it that much larger. Exponentially larger.

Face it, you're surrounded by many more possibilities for growth than you realize. All it takes is improving — adding zeros — to things that can be measured because **what gets measured improves.**

Once you start measuring something, you unconsciously try to improve it because you're watching it.

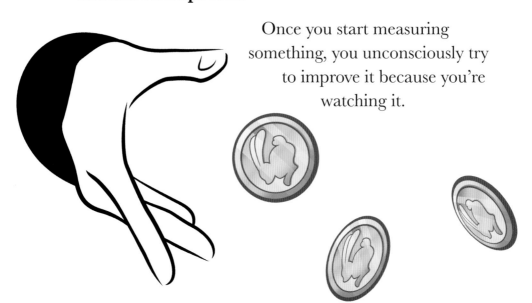

That's what we wanted to give you in this book, a sharp level of awareness methodically broken into 5 easy-to-understand disciplines that enable you to see things about your business you could not see before, or maybe were unwilling to acknowledge. The self-guided assessment helped you understand whether you're serving your constituents as you should, and which disciplines need support. We then gave you definitive action steps to improve on what's already working well and build up what needs help.

Used regularly, the information in this book can maintain what you need to achieve sustainable and exponential growth by satisfying your 5 constituent groups. We designed it as a handbook so that everyone in your company, from CEO to stock clerk, can find solutions in it as challenges are identified. They all benefit from clearly understanding how everyone contributes to the magic your company creates.

Understanding how everyone working together creates magic is our goal for your company. We hope it's yours, too. When everyone involved agrees on a definition of success that makes sense for the business and then develops a plan with realistic timing and goals that make it happen, you create magic for yourselves and your constituents.

Over the years, we've worked with thousands of successful companies who do just that, and we've found they all have a disciplined approach that enables them to devote thousands of hours to the following:

- the things that will make them succeed;

- reaching a common goal with a high level of excitement and commitment;

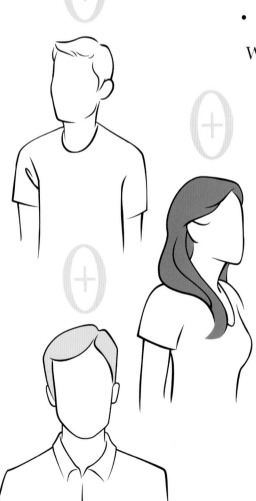

- adding value to their clear niche in the marketplace;

- a higher purpose than just profit.

We realize that not everyone can pick up a handbook, follow action plans, and achieve the results we know are possible. Learning new behaviors can be challenging, especially when there are other demands on resources. We also know that because the process is not a quick one, it may take a while to tell whether the steps you're taking are the best for your current situation, and the risk of possibly wasting time may seem to outweigh any benefit from adding zeros.

We hope that after reading this book you're convinced your business has the potential for exponential growth even if you're not entirely sure how to achieve it. We're reasonably certain we've laid out the arguments that show that making even small changes can lead to optimal success, and we'd like to help you reach that success.

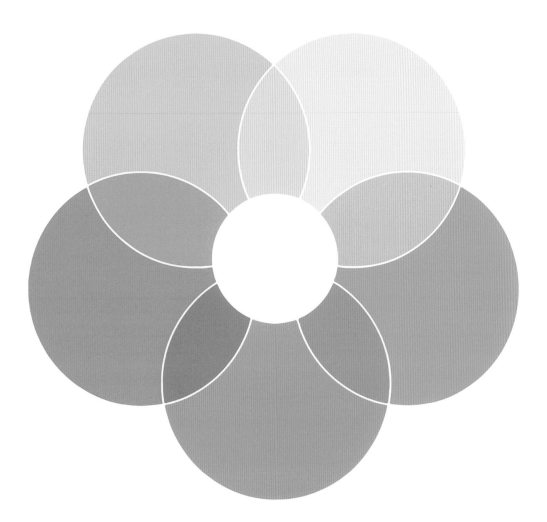

GLOSSARY

Scarcity Mentality. A Scarcity Mentality is the belief that resources are always inadequate.

Business Strategy. A business strategy is an articulation of the way a company does business. It consists of two parts: where the business wants to go (its goals), and the roadmap that gets it there (the plan).

Business Sustainability. A result of predictability in assessing the market and growth. Predictability creates sustainability, and predictability comes from understanding the causes of past growth to calculate future exponential growth.

Business Stability. A company that is stable has high employee morale; a very high staff retention rate; customers and employees who are treated with equal respect.

Business Consistency. A business demonstrates consistency when customers enjoy the same experience with every member of the team; everyone does what they say they'll do; employees have responsibility for their roles and are confident in their abilities; the company is proactive and one step ahead of the competition; the company is always looking for a better way to do things, and the company demonstrates financial confidence and stability. A business is consistent when it forecasts a positive economic outlook for the months ahead; its processes and efficiencies show constant improvement; and it practices good management with no micro-management.

Business Development. Business development is about attracting the right client, servicing the right client, and having high client retention through great customer satisfaction and loyalty. Successful businesses don't want everyone to be their customer, so they target the specific people who are the best match for the business. This makes it easier to satisfy those customers and makes it likely that they'll be willing to recommend the company to their friends.

Engaged Management. Engaged management provides the tools that employees need, namely, clear processes that lead to success, the skills for those processes, well-defined metrics for what is expected of them, detailed plans for development and advancement, and, above all, communication. People don't leave companies; they leave their managers. To employees, the manager is the company because she is what they see and experience. If the manager doesn't satisfy the employees, they aren't engaged with the company, turning in poor work and eventually leaving. A really great manager practically becomes transparent, enabling employees to see the whole company. A really great manager is also a great leader.

Discipline of Execution. Doing the right things in the right order by the right people, leading to consistent results — no magical intervention necessary.

Discipline of Strategy. No matter how old the company is, its strategy enables it to continually reinvent itself, so that it's sustainable.

Discipline of Business Development. Use cues and clues from the past to create predictability so there is no need to make wild guesses about the future.

Discipline of People. This ensures that when a team of skilled workers has proper leadership instead of being left to its own devices, the company gains stability.

Discipline of Mission. This creates an emotional connection between the company and the people it serves, one that is personally satisfying while amplifying an individual's ability to make the world a better place.

Constituent. The constituents are the company, the customer, the team member, the stakeholder, and the community – What every organization must satisfy in order to build exponential growth.

Opportunity. In business, opportunity is the demand or market need that your company can fill.

Marketability. The likelihood that a product or service will sell.

Leverage: Using what you have to get more.

Scalability: The ability to maintain or improve profit margins while sales volume increases.

Franchising. Franchising is a method for expanding a business and distributing goods and services through a contract relationship. Franchisors specify the products and services offered by their franchisees and provide them with an operating system, brand, and support.

Licensing. Licensing is used for the sale of products when a company has invented or developed a product or process and then protected it by a patent, copyright, or trademark. Another party may seek access to the product or process to advance their own business. An owner may also grant a license when someone else wants to use an established business name; the licensor receives a royalty as compensation and retains ownership of the intellectual property.

Predictability. This is every marketer's dream. The ultimate goal of a marketer is predicting a business's future based on proven marketing techniques, a sales process, and second-to-none customer service. You create predictability by testing and measuring for a period of time and then analyzing the data that produces. This allows you to know whether the actions you take are giving the results you need. When you know what action produces which results, you have reasonable certainty about how to have the future you want.

Marketing Plan. A marketing plan is a comprehensive document describing what a business will do to accomplish specific objectives within a specified period. It outlines how, when, and how often the company will get its message in front of its core customers.

Branding. Branding is everything a company does. Branding extends down to the smallest details that make a company stand out and differentiates it from its competition.

Pricing. The cost of your service. Your pricing should reflect the confidence and benefit you bring to your customer. Customers are willing to pay more for excellent service and perceived value, so it makes sense to provide that value at an optimal price, creatively educating and communicating to your customers that you are offering much more than a perceived commodity.

Lead Generation. Generating leads is the process of collecting lots of data about potential consumers and analyzing it to find potential sales.

Core Customer. Your core customer is the person most likely to buy your product or service in the quantity required for optimal profit.

Buyer Persona. The demographics and psychographics of your customers can be combined to create your core customer's buyer persona: a detailed description of who they are and what motivates them to buy.

Sales Playbook. A proper sales process first guides salespeople to determine if a prospective buyer represents the company's core customer. Then the sales process gauges whether the potential customer will be happy with their purchase. This process leads to high conversion rates.

Customer Service. Customer service is a mindset that places the needs of the customer above your own at all times. An attitude of gratitude reminds everyone that the company appreciates the customer's business. A mindset centered on appreciation is positive and proactive, making it easy for people to do business with you.

KPIs – Key Performance Indicators. Sustainable businesses use numbers such as ROI to identify the actions that create results. They do this by creating Key Performance Indicators for each department and each position in that area. The KPIs are used to measure progress, comparing today's results with yesterday's and with the projections for tomorrow.

ROI – Return on Investment. ROI is a ratio between the net profit and cost of investment resulting from an investment of some resources. Return on investment is a performance measure used by businesses to identify the efficiency of an investment or number of different investments.

Net Promoter Score. The Net Promoter Score (NPS) is a system that rates loyalty by determining how many customers are Promoters, Detractors, or Passives. Promoters are loyal customers who say they'll recommend the company to their family and friends. Detractors are those who are unlikely to recommend the company, and may even speak against it. Passives are satisfied in general but could just as well do business with someone else.

Leadership. The art of creating passionate and focused people.

Talent Development. This is helping everyone who works for the organization, from top management to frontline employees, continually developing and improving the hard and soft skills needed for short-term and long-term goals. It's a fundamental value for any company.

Recruitment. Finding the people who not only make your success possible but inevitable. A clear hiring and recruitment process is well-documented, with well-defined steps to follow each time a new team member needs to be hired. It's designed to bring in the people who are a perfect fit for the company in general, and the job in particular.

DISC. The DISC behavioral profile is a system of behavior analysis that can be used to predict a person's behavior when they work alone or with others. It's useful for identifying a person's primary behavior type among four possible categories: Dominant, Influential, Steady, Compliant. Dominant behavior types enjoy competition and challenge. They're goal-oriented and want others to recognize them for their efforts and achievements. Influential behavior types are very interested in meeting and being with people. They are optimistic, outgoing, and socially skilled, and are quick at establishing relationships. Steady behavior types are usually patient, calm and controlled. They are very willing to help others, particularly those they consider friends. Compliant behavior types are detail and process-oriented. They are cautious rather than impulsive and avoid taking risks.

Process. Without documented processes in place, a business relies entirely on the skills of the workers who produce the best work. A process is a sequence of interdependent, linked procedures which, at every stage, consume one or more resources (employee time, energy, machines, money) to convert inputs (data, material, parts, etc.) into outputs. These outputs then serve as inputs for the next stage until a known goal or result is reached.

Management. Not to be confused with Leadership. Management oversees processes so the team is competent and productive. Proper management balances processes and people, efficiency and humanity, without jeopardizing either one.

Big, Hairy, Audacious Goal. (BHAG) A 10+ year goal that causes the business to think and act differently.

Brad Sugars, Co - Author

Brad Sugars is the Founder and Chairman of ActionCOACH, the world's Number One business coaching firm, with more than 1000 offices in 77 countries. ActionCOACH provides weekly training to over 15,000 companies.

In addition to being a successful entrepreneur and dedicated family man, he is also a bestselling author of 16 acclaimed business books (including four international best sellers). Brad has taught over a million people worldwide how to create business, real estate, and financial success.

Monte Wyatt, Co - Author

Monte is one of the top business coaches in ActionCOACH Business Coaching and brings over 20 years of leadership and personal development experience to executives and business owners. He coaches CEOs and business owners to improve their business through greater awareness, education of proven strategies and tactics, implementation and execution, and finally discipline to stay focused on their goals.

In addition to coaching executives & business owners one - on - one, Monte conducts public and private workshops and seminars. His goal is to help executives and business owners reach their full potential.

About Adding Zeros - The Company

Adding Zeros is a company that works with executives to achieve exponential growth helping them grow in multiples rather than small percentage increases.

Adding Zeros provides companies the tools and the guidance to add zeros in every aspect of the business – revenue, margin, profit, customer acquisition, customer retention, employee engagement, employee retention, and community involvement.

It is our purpose to create profitable corporate citizenship in mid - market companies worldwide. Through executive development and 12 - week facilitated programs, Adding Zeros provides proven structure, wholistic content, training, and support to exponentially growth - minded coaches, trainers, consultants and mid - market businesses.

Is Your Company Ready to Achieve Exponential Growth?

If you are an executive that wants to begin to instill the 5 Disciplines into your organization, then visit PullingProfits. com.

On this website you will find all the information you need to determine which 12 - week executive program or executive development service will meet your company's needs and goals.

While you are visiting, you can purchase:

- The 5 Disciplines Team Assessment

- Download white papers

- Read case studies

- Discover what other executives

  are saying about us

- Further your mastery of

  the 5 Disciplines

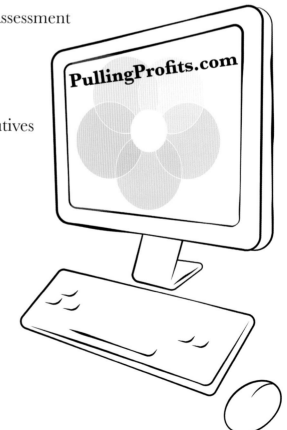

PullingProfits.com

About Our 12 - week Executive Programs

Adding Zeros 12 - week programs are foundational for executives that seek to foster the 5 Disciplines in their companies. These programs are not for those looking for quick fix training, but for serious executives that wish to add zeros by enacting lasting company - wide change.

Each 12 - week program includes materials and a weekly 1 - hour on - site session. Each session is facilitated by a trained and certified Adding Zeros facilitator who will guide you through proven processes that will instill the disciplines your company needs to best serve your constituents and grow your company by multiples, not increments.

The Discipline of Mission
12 - week Executive Program

You company's mission is not a statement on a plaque. It is about your deeper values. It is about how we treat each other, treat our customers, and how we make decisions. And these values must be behaviorally based so everyone knows how to act every single day. These values also fuel the passion people will have for the company, inside and out.

The three areas of Mission are Core Values, Purpose, and Giving Back. In this program, executives will evaluate their current business condition in this discipline and create short - term and long - term actions to advance each area throughout the organization.

The Discipline of Strategy
12 - Week Executive Program

This 12 - week program will guide executives on how to add zeros in the areas of organizational longevity and sustainability. In order to be sustainable a company must have a clear strategy that defines how your company will win. Winning isn't about today's margin, profit, or revenue. It is about outlasting your competition long - term.

The four areas of Strategy are: Opportunity, Leverage, Scalability, and Marketability. In this program executives will evaluate their current business condition in this discipline and create short - term and long - term actions to advance each area throughout the organization.

The Strategy of Business Development
12 - Week Executive Program

No business can survive long term with roller coaster sales and this 12 - week program guides executives on how to add zeros and predictability in the areas of sales and customer retention.

Predictability is the result of outstanding business development that attracts a specific audience that will buy your product and services again and again. The three areas of Business Development are: Marketing, Sales, and Customer Service, and participants will evaluate their current business condition in this discipline and create short - term and long - term actions to advance each area company - wide.

addingZEROS

The Discipline of People
12 - Week Executive Program

A great company's stability derives from employee retention and high employee engagement. Great companies have both management and leadership. Leadership creates passion and focus with team members.

This 12 - week program will give executives an education, understanding, and action plan on the areas of Leadership, Talent Development, and Recruitment. Executives will evaluate their current business condition in the discipline of People and create short - term and long - term actions to advance stability and add zeros throughout the organization.

The Discipline of Execution
12 - week Executive Program

Great Execution breeds consistency inside and outside of your organization. No matter who a customer interacts with they should receive consistent messages and experiences. By implementing and following proven processes and routines as an organization you become consistent in the eyes of customers and your constituents.

Executives in this program will discover more about Process, Management, and the Financial Controls needed to maintain consistency company - wide. Executives will evaluate their current business condition in this discipline and create short term and long - term actions to create more consistency

The 5 Disciplines of Exponential Growth
12 - Week Executive Program

You and your team of executives will receive an overview of education, understanding, and an action plan for better serving the 5 Constituents every business must satisfy (Company, Customer, Team, Stakeholders, and the Community) and how to implement the 5 Disciplines: Strategy, Business Development, People, Execution, and Mission into the organization.

This program will help your company enact better company - wide discipline in the areas of revenue, margin, profit, customer acquisition, customer retention, employee engagement, employee retention, and community involvement.